W9-BOM-376

THE EATING AND DRINKING SERIES

•

"...an opinionated little compendium."
~ New York Times

"...irresistible little guide."
~ Chicago Tribune

"an elegant, small guide..."
~ Minneapolis Star Tribune

"Makes dining easy and enjoyable."
~ Toronto Sun

"...a terrific primer for first-time visitors."
~ Houston Chronicle

"...opening up the world of good eating with their innovative paperback series."
~ Salt Lake Tribune

"...travelers who know their cervelle *(brains) from* cervelle de canut *(herbed cheese spread)."*
~ USA Today

"It's written as if a friend were talking to you."
~ Celebrity Chef Tyler Florence

ABOUT THE AUTHORS

Andy Herbach is a lawyer. Michael Dillon is a graphic designer. Both authors reside in Milwaukee, Wisconsin. They are the authors of *Eating and Drinking in Paris*, *Eating and Drinking in Italy*, *Eating and Drinking in Spain* and *Eating and Drinking in Latin America*. Andy is the author of several books published by Open Road, including *Best of Paris*, *Best of Provence and the French Riviera*, and *Best of Spain*.

You can e-mail comments, additions and corrections to eatndrink@aol.com.

UPDATES

Updates to this guide can be found on the message board at www.eatndrink.com.

ACKNOWLEDGMENTS
French editor: Mme. Marie Fossier
English editors: Jonathan Stein and Marian Olson
Contributors: Mark Berry, Evelyn Coulon, Jay Filter, Jeff Kurz, Loralyn Lasoued, Trish Medalen, Terry Medalen, Jim Mortell and Dan Schmidt
This fourth edition has been updated by Andy Herbach.
Andy thanks Karl Raaum for all his help.

EATING AND DRINKING IN

Paris

Menu Translator and Restaurant Guide

Andy Herbach

OPEN ROAD PUBLISHING

OPEN ROAD PUBLISHING

Your passport to the perfect trip!

Open Road Publishing
P.O. Box 284
Cold Spring Harbor, NY 11724

www.openroadguides.com

Fourth edition

Illustrations by Michael Dillon
Updated by Andy Herbach

Library of Congress Control No. 2007942830
ISBN-10: 1-59360-111-5
ISBN-13: 978-1-59360-111-9

Contents

EATING AND DRINKING IN PARIS

 AN INTRODUCTION

When you think of Paris, you may think of the Eiffel Tower, the Louvre or the Champs-Elysées. When we think of Paris, the first thing that comes to mind is food.

Of course, every traveler has a different set of desires and expectations: rest and relaxation, shopping, exploring, hiking, reading...whatever. For us, the making of a memorable vacation begins and ends with food. Not that we don't like and appreciate museums, gardens, shopping – okay, we hate shopping – but we do enjoy jogging along the Seine and doing normal tourist things like exploring medieval churches. And sure, the Louvre is great, but have you had one of those long, skinny French hot dogs the vendors sell on the streets outside? Honestly, we can't remember if we saw the Mona Lisa, but that hot dog, covered with shredded Swiss cheese, grilled golden brown and then slathered with Dijon mustard, was exquisite and remains a cherished memory of a visit to Paris.

Beyond the simple pleasures of eating, dining in a foreign country gives you an insight into the soul of its people. It's a glimpse of their customs, their likes and dislikes, their foibles, their accomplishments. It puts you in contact with local culture. In fact, for most travelers, the closest they will come to actually interacting with real live natives is when they are eating in a restaurant and speaking to waiters and bartenders. While we probably wouldn't count them as close friends, there are waiters who remember us and who have made our meals more enjoyable simply through their personal interactions with us.

If you love to travel as we do, you know the importance of a good guide. Dining, like traveling, requires the same. A good guide can make the difference between a memorable evening and a nightmare or maybe just a dull one, but who wants a dull evening when they're on vacation? There is nothing worse than hiking all over a city looking for a good place to eat dinner, finding nothing, in near panic settling for whatever comes along next, having a lousy meal, then, upon leaving, discovering what looks like the best restaurant in the world right around the corner. Believe us, it happens all the time. The restaurant-guide portion of our book is a quick list of some of our favorite places in Paris, and the menu-translator section will help you find your way around a menu written in French. It gives you the freedom to fearlessly enter places you might never have entered before and order a dinner without shouting, pointing, or hand waving. This book also contains an alphabetical listing of food and drink commonly found on menus in Paris.

Eating & Drinking in Paris isn't so much about food and wine. It's really about easing the process of ordering food and having a good time – or at least not a stressful time – doing it. Our guide was created for the not-so-daring traveler who wants to enjoy and experience authentic cuisine and know what he or she is eating.

OUR MISSION

As silly as it might sound, we have one:

No Menus in English.

Aside from, say, in England.

We want people to eat in restaurants without English menus. We don't like to see the United States when we're visiting France; we want foreign when we're on foreign soil. When we visited Athens we were horrified to see a gigantic neon-and-plastic, two-story Kenny Rogers Roast Chicken franchise on Syntagma Square right smack across from the Greek Parliament. On the beautiful port of Marigot on the island of St. Martin in the French West Indies, a single Kentucky Fried Chicken put all of the small, locally owned and picturesque grill shacks, called *lolos*, out of business, virtually destroying what was charming about the port. We have nothing against fast food, but when we're in France, we want it to look French. We don't want to see the golden arches under the Eiffel Tower (they tried to do that...seriously) and we don't want to see a menu in English. As we see it, a menu in English is the first step in the Americanization of the restaurants of the world, the first domino. And once it's not foreign, what's the point of going?

 ABOUT EATING AND DRINKING IN PARIS

No other city in the world has a greater number of places to eat per square mile than Paris. Nowhere else can you find the variety, the charm, the sheer joy and celebration of food. And nowhere else can you be more intimidated trying to get fed. Parisians observe all kinds of decorum about their food. They have many, many types of eating establishments which to us is confusing. What's wrong with calling them all restaurants? They eat in a nearly ritualistic manner, and want you to do so as well. As Americans we feel we are often blundering into a private party and haven't received all the pertinent information. The following is some of that information.

THE MENU A menu is a fixed-price meal, not that piece of paper listing the food items. If you want what we consider a menu, you need to ask for *la carte*. The menu is almost always posted on the front of the restaurant so you know what you're getting into, both foodwise and pricewise, before you enter. The fixed-price daily menu (*menu fixe*) will generally include several choices for each of 2 or 3 courses. The daily fixed-price menu is cheaper than ordering off the menu (*carte*). Our American term *à la carte* means 'of the menu,' in case you hadn't noticed.

Restaurants frequently offer a plate of the day (*plat du jour*), and some restaurants offer a set-price gourmet menu (*menu dégustation*) of specialties of the chef. The price of a meal will occasionally include the house wine (*vin compris*).

A simple green salad (*salade verte*) is occasionally served with or sometimes after the main course, before the cheese course or dessert. Rarely is this type of salad even listed on the menu. Larger, more involved–and to us what seem like full meals–salads such as *roquefort*, *lardons* and *endive* are usually listed as first courses or *entrées*. However, times have changed and you may now order a green salad as an appetizer but you will most likely have to ask for it, because, as we said earlier, you won't find it on the menu.

An *entrée* is a first course, the *plat* is the main course, followed by cheese and then dessert. Coffee is served at the end – never with your meal. There are all sorts of coffees that you can order decaffeinated which, if your meal is ending at midnight, as so often happens in Paris, you might want to consider. Ask for *déca* which rhymes with day-cah. You'll find a list of the different types of coffees on page 64.

WHY IS THERE A DOG AT THE TABLE NEXT TO ME? Parisians really love their dogs. It is not uncommon (no matter what type of eating establishment you are dining in) to find several dogs under tables, or even on their own chairs.

ASKING FOR YOUR BILL The bill in a restaurant is called *l'addition*...but the bill in a bar is called *le compte* or *la note*; confusing? It's easier if you just make a scribbling motion with your fingers on the palm of your hand.

TIPPING A service charge is almost always added to your bill in Paris. Depending on the service, it is sometimes appropriate to leave an additional 5 to 10%. The menu will usually note that service is included (*service compris*). Sometimes this is abbreviated with the letters s.c. The letters s.n.c. stand for *service non compris*; this means that the service is not included in the price, and you must leave a tip.

You will sometimes find *couvert* or cover charge on your menu (a small charge just for placing your butt at the table).

MEALTIMES In Paris, lunch is served from noon to around 2:00 p.m., and dinner from 8:00 p.m. to 11:00 p.m. Restaurants usually have two seatings: at 8:00 or 8:30 p.m., and at 10:00 or 10:30 p.m. The restaurant will be less crowded at the early seating, but don't worry, it will fill up fast.

RESERVATIONS It's advisable if you're visiting a restaurant (as opposed to a *bistro* or *café*) to have reservations. Although you might see an empty restaurant and assume there will be seats available, most places we have listed will be full by 8:00 p.m. – with people who have made reservations. We advise making reservations in person. We like to do a walk-by in the afternoon, stop in and make reservations. Don't be afraid. The word for reservation is the same in English and French. You can do times and numbers with your fingers. If you speak a little French, you can do it on the phone. The problem with phoning, however, comes when, after you've said in a timid voice that you would like to make reservations if possible, they ask you a question in rapid-fire French and at that pace asking what your name is sounds pretty much like how many people are in the party or what time were you thinking about eating. Be patient; eventually you'll get the idea across.

WATER Europeans joke that you can tell a U.S. tourist from his "fanny pack," clothes and ubiquitous bottle of mineral water. Tap water is safe in Paris. Occasionally, you will find *non potable* signs in restrooms. This means that the water is not safe for drinking.

Waiters and waitresses often bring *eau minérale* (mineral water) to your table. You will be charged for it, so if you don't want mineral water ask for *une carafe d'eau* or *eau du robinet* (tap water).

WHAT TO DO WHEN NOTHING SEEMS TO BE OPEN Sundays can be frustrating. Nothing seems to be open. You can phone in advance but that isn't necessarily going to work because the place might not be open when you call.
The best thing to do is to go to an area where there is a high concentration of restaurants. We have some of them listed on page 16.

10

We think of most of these places as restaurants. We have a hard time seeing the differences between many of these establishments. Cafés seem like bars, bistros seem like brasseries, and they all seem like restaurants. What some people think of as a limited menu can seem complete to someone else (like us). Our full list of restaurants starting on page 19 includes cafés, brasseries, bistros and restaurants.

Alimentation: A small food store.

Auberge: An inn serving food and drink. These are most often found in the country, but restaurants in Paris also use the name. One favorite is Auberge Pyrénnées-Cévennes (see the restaurant section).

Bar à café: Coffee shop serving light meals. Don't be misled by the name, though, as they rarely serve alcohol.

Bistro: Smaller and less fashionable than a restaurant, serving traditional, simple French food. Some are very similar to taverns or pubs.

Bar à champagne: Champagne bar.

Bar à vin: Wine bar.

Boucherie: Butcher's shop.

Boulangerie: Bakery. Nowhere else on earth can you get *baguettes* that taste like they do in France. Bread is often offered *bien cuit* (crusty) or *bien tendre* (doughy). Many *boulangeries* also sell sandwiches, tarts, quiches and small pizzas.

Brasserie: Originally, this term referred to a beer hall, but today serves food and drink.

Buffet: Eating establishment usually found in railroad stations.

Cabaret: Dinner and a show.

Café: Simple café dining is one of the pleasures of a trip to Paris. You can learn more sitting in a café for an hour than spending the day in a museum. In Paris, people-watching is like no other place in the world. Cafés serve alcoholic beverages and snacks. Some serve complete meals.

Cave: Cellar. This also refers to a wine shop. See Vins et Alcools.

Charcuteries: Originally these were pork butchers selling pork, ham, sausages, *jambon de Paris* and sometimes chicken. Now, most are delicatessens with prepared salads, quiches and other food tarts.

Chevaline: Horse-meat butcher's shop. These shops are becoming few and far between, but have a small and devoted clientele. Usually, there is a horse-head emblem on the front of the shop.

Chocolaterie: Chocolate shop.

Confiserie: Sweet shop.

Crémerie: Cream (and cheese) shop.

Crêperies: Popular for lunch, serving *crêpes* (thin filled pancakes).

Emporter: Carry-out foods.

Épicerie: Grocer's shop (literally "spice shop").

Express: Any establishment with this name is usually a snack bar.

Fromagerie: Serves up to 400 official types of cheese.

Glaces et Sorbets/Glacier: Ice cream & sorbet shop.

Berthillon

4th/Métro Pont-Marie

31 rue Saint-Louis-en-I'lle (on the Île St-Louis)

Tel. 01/43.54.31.61

Closed Mon., Tue. and Aug.

Tourists and Parisians alike line up at the carry-out window for the best-known ice cream in Paris. Over thirty flavors from *chocolat blanc* (white chocolate) to *pain d'épice* (gingerbread). It's on one of the most beautiful streets in all of Paris.

Hostellerie: Upscale country restaurant.

Marché: Market.

Marchand de Légumes: Vegetable shop.

Pâtisseries: Pastry shops. The Parisian favorite of *baba au rhum* (spongecake soaked in rum) was invented at **Stohrer**, 2nd/Métro Les Halles, 51 rue Montorgueil, Tel. 01/42.33.38.20, Closed part of Aug.

Pizzerias: You can figure this one out yourself.

Poissonnerie: Seafood shop.

Relais: Country inn or restaurant.

Restaurant: See our separate section on recommended restaurants.

Restoroute: Restaurant found on the highway.

Rôtisserie: Restaurant that usually specializes in roasted and grilled meats, especially chicken.

Salon de Thé: Open mid-morning to late evening, serving light fare, salads, cakes, ice cream and, of course, *thé* (tea).

Tabac: Bars where you can also buy cigarettes (they are, in fact, the only places in France where you can buy tobacco), stamps, tickets for public transportation, lottery tickets and phone cards. They are often also *cafés*.

Traiteur: Delicatessen (this can also mean caterer). There seem to be Indo-Chinese and Italian traiteurs all over the place. The food is usually good and inexpensive.

Triperie: Tripe shop.

Vins et Alcools: Wine and liquor shop.

Volailler: Poultry shop.

Even people who speak passable French can have trouble reading a menu. The grand-sounding *suprême de volaille* is simply a chicken breast. *Cervelle* is brains, but *cervelle de canut* is an herbed cheese spread from Lyon.

Remember that the dish that you ordered may not be exactly as described in this guide. Every chef is (and should be) innovative. What we have listed for you in this guide is the most common version of a dish.

Times can change and restaurants can close, so do a walk-by earlier in the day or the day before, if possible.

Each of our recommended restaurants offers something different. Some have great food and little ambiance. Others have great ambiance and adequate food. Still others have both. Our goal is to find restaurants that are moderately priced and enjoyable. All restaurants have been tried and tested. Not enough can be said for a friendly welcome and great service. No matter how fabulous the meal, the experience will always be better when the staff treats you as if they actually want you there rather than simply tolerating your presence.

Be careful, menus in English are often wrong.

Tips for Budget Dining in Paris There is no need to spend a lot of money in Paris to have good food. Of course it helps when the euro is weaker than the dollar, but there are all kinds of fabulous foods to be had inexpensively all over Paris.

Eat at a neighborhood restaurant or bistro. You'll always know the price of a meal before entering, as almost all Paris restaurants post the menu and prices in the window. Never order anything whose price is not known in advance. If you see *selon grosseur* (sometimes abbreviated as s/g) this means that you are paying by weight, which can be extremely expensive.

Delis, *traiteurs* and food stores can provide cheap and wonderful meals. Buy some cheese, bread, wine and other snacks and have a picnic in one of Paris's great parks. In fact, no matter what, you should go into a *boulangerie* and buy a *baguette* at least once. Remember to pack a corkscrew and eating utensils when you leave home.

Lunch, even at the most expensive restaurants listed in this guide, always has a lower fixed price. So, have lunch as your main meal.

Restaurants and bistros that have menus written in English (especially those near tourist attractions) are almost always more expensive than neighborhood restaurants and bistros.

Large department stores frequently have supermarkets in the basement and restaurants that have reasonably priced food. The ultimate grocery store (with wine cellar and carry-out) is **La Grande Épicerie** located in Au Bon Marché department store (7th/Métro Sèvres-Babylone, 38 rue de Sèvres, closed Sun.). Don't miss it! It's also interesting to visit the supermarkets in **Monoprix**, the discount department store chain. Not at all like at home!

Street vendors generally sell inexpensive and terrific food; you'll find excellent hot dogs, *crêpes* and roast-chicken sandwiches all over Paris. At lunch time, you'll see Parisians eating long, thin *baguettes* filled with chicken, mayonnaise and sliced eggs throughout the city.

And, for the cost of a cup of coffee or a drink, you can linger at a café and watch the world pass you by for as long as you want. It's one of Paris's greatest bargains.

Kids love **Hippopotamus**, a chain of inexpensive restaurants with many locations in Paris. They have noisy televisions everywhere, paper table covers for coloring (they provide crayons), and balloons (everything you thought you'd left behind at home).

And don't eat at McDonald's, for God's sake.

FOOD MARKETS AND OTHER PLACES TO FIND FOOD

If nothing else, food markets are very interesting. Though you may feel intimidated by the wild goings-on (not to mention the sights and smells) it is absolutely worth a trip to see a real outdoor Parisian market. Filled with colorful vendors, stinky cheese, fresh produce, poultry and hanging rabbits, this is real Paris at its most diverse and beautiful. Parisians still shop (some every day) at food markets around the city. Unless noted otherwise, all are open Tuesday through noon on Sunday. Some of the best-known are:

Rue Montorgueil, 1st/Métro Les Halles
Rue Mouffetard, 5th/Métro Censier-Daubenton
Rue de Buci, 6th/Métro Mabillon
Marché Raspail, 6th/Métro Rennes (open Sunday) (organic)
Rue Cler, 7th/Métro École Militaire
Marché Bastille on the boulevard Richard Lenoir,
   11th/Métro Bastille (open Thursday and Sunday)
Rue Daguerre, 14th/Métro Denfert-Rochereau
Rue Poncelet, 17th/Métro Ternes

Markets are places that you might appreciate as you would a museum, but there are other places around Paris where you can also see and experience food in a unique setting. The area around the Place de la Madeleine (8th/Métro Madeleine) is packed with fabulous specialty food shops (the windows of the food store **Fauchon** are worth a trip by themselves), wine dealers, restaurants, and tea rooms. This is a perfect place for eating and purchasing culinary souvenirs. There is something for every taste – but

15

this is an upscale area, and can be expe┆ sive. In addition to food markets and ┆special-ty shops, there are several┆ areas in Paris where many resta┆urants are concentrated in small p┆ckets. These are areas that are charming ju┆ t in and of themselves, nice to walk thr┆ugh and nice to eat in, particularly outside c┆ a nice evening.

┆ea is on rue Pot-de-Fer between la rue To┆ ┆efort ┆tard, just off the market. It's a slip of a str┆et but it's ┆ng restaurants with clothed tables set for dinner, ┆ging from the roof overhangs, and a uniquely ┆ (Métro Monge).

┆ is *not* the Passage Brady in the 10th arrondisse-m┆ ┆er the narrow *passage* around 33 boulevard Strasbourg and find mostly Indian, but also Turkish and Moroccan, restaurants in an interestingly Indian setting. These are inexpensive restaurants in a working-class neighborhood, and the passage, while exotic in many ways, is not upscale (Métro Château d'Eau).

There are several restaurants and bars on the lovely Place Sainte-Catherine (enter from rue Caron off of rue St-Antoine) in the Marais. Overlooking the square is **Soprano**, serving delicious authentic Italian dishes. Tel. 01/42.72.37.21. The Place Sainte-Catherine is a special, quiet respite in this fashionable area (Métro St-Paul).

You'll find loads of restaurants off of la rue Saint-Jacques in the area around la rue Saint-Séverin and la rue de la Huchette in the 5th. This area, a short walk from Notre Dame, is filled with French, Italian, Greek and other restaurants jammed into small streets. It's a very pleasant walk, and you're bound to find somewhere to eat. Nearby in the 6th is the cour du Commerce, a tiny alleyway off of la rue St-André-des-Arts, which is lined with restaurants to fit all pocketbooks (Métros Saint-Michel, Odéon or Cluny-La Sorbonne).

TEN SIMPLE RULES

1. Avoid eating in a restaurant that has a menu written in English. In case you haven't gathered, we're against them for a number of reasons. One good reason is that at one restaurant, we were automatically given the English menu (which is really irritating, since we hate being so obviously American) and we discovered as we walked out that it bore no relationship to the French menu which was more than twice as long.

2. Don't be afraid. They can't and won't hurt you. They are not laughing at you, they don't dislike you, they aren't even thinking about you. Waiters in France are trained professionals whose job is to serve you. Despite what you've heard, they want you to have a good time. Sometimes they are just mystified by what we do.

When asked what the French think about Thanksgiving Julia Child replied, "The French aren't thinking about Thanksgiving, they're focused on themselves." Which pretty much sums it up.

3. Don't ever call the waiter "*garçon*." Though sometimes in bars a Parisian will use this word, travelers should never use it.

4. Try to make reservations. This isn't as difficult as it seems; the words are similar in both languages and they'll get the gist of what you're trying to do. We often do a walk-by in the afternoon and stop in to make the reservation. When we go back that night they are almost always happy to see us again.

5. Return to a restaurant if you like it. If you have the luxury of time and can withstand the temptation to try other restaurants, you will always be treated better if they recognize you. Few travelers return to the same restaurant.

6. Parisians dine leisurely. Don't expect to get the same speed of service as at home. For the French, dinner is nearly a ritual. In its full-blown form, it begins with an *apéritif*. This is often accompanied

by an *amuse-gueule*, a little snack of some sort. After this, you order an *hors-d'oeuvre*. Then comes an *entrée*, which is a first course – *pâté* or a composed salad, such as a salad with shrimp or hard-boiled eggs – and then the main course which will most likely be meat or fish. The main course is sometimes accompanied by or followed by a salad, but it is a simple green salad. After this, just when you think you're going to explode and have secretly unbuckled your belt, the *serveur* arrives with selections from the cheese platter that are followed by dessert, and, finally, coffee. But if you do not want to follow the French protocol, don't. Even if the waiter seems to disapprove, do what you like.

7. Don't talk loudly. You will notice that the French speak softly, Americans don't; we just can't help it. But believe us: Those loud voices coupled with running shoes, backpacks, "fanny packs," large, conspicuous guide books and cameras are like wearing a neon sign announcing that you are a tourist, an American tourist.

8. Stand your ground without being aggressive. In the years we've been traveling, it seems that waiters have become more relaxed about the rituals of eating, and will accommodate you if you insist on what you want – within reason, of course.

9. Visit a street vendor at least once in Paris. Whether it's sandwiches, hot dogs or *crêpes*, Parisian street vendors sell delicious "food on the run." Do yourself a favor, and sample some.

10. Always be courteous. Remember that you are a guest in their country. There are simple things that the French do that we don't, like excusing yourself or saying please all the time.

S'il vous plaît (seel voo play) after nearly everything is a safe way to be very polite. Seriously. A polite Parisian ALWAYS finishes a greeting (such as *bonjour* – hello) or affirmation (such as *oui* – yes) with a title. Thus, *bonjour* is always *bonjour, madame* or *m'sieur* and yes or no is always *oui, m'sieur* or *madame*. And just so you know, you say *bonjour*, which is essentially hello, all day and night. *Bonsoir* – good evening – is reserved for leaving and after 7:00 p.m., and *bonne nuit* – good night – is only used when you are actually on your way to bed.

PLACES TO EAT

RESTAURANTS, BISTROS, BRASSERIES
CAFÉS AND SALONS DE THÉ

Phone numbers, days closed and hours of operation often change, so it's advisable to check ahead. Restaurants in tourist areas may have different hours and days of operation during low season. Reservations are recommended for all restaurants unless noted. The telephone country code for France is 33. When calling within France you must dial the area code. The area code for Paris is 01. However, you do not use the 0 before the area code when calling France from the U.S. or Canada. Confused?

Oui m'sieur?
Combien
de personnes?

Here's what it looks like:

From the United States:
(011) 33 1/43.26.48.23

From within Paris:
01/43.26.48.23

Prices are for a main course and without wine.
Lunch, even at the most expensive restaurants listed below, always has a lower fixed price. Credit cards accepted unless noted.

Inexpensive: under 10 euros
Moderate: 11 - 20 euros
Expensive: 21 - 30 euros
Very Expensive: over 30 euros

Allard

6th/Métro Odéon
41 rue St-André-des-Arts
Tel. 01/43.26.48.23
Closed Sun. & part of Aug.
Diners repeatedly praise the food at this
typical Parisian bistro. The signature dish is
canard aux olives (duck roasted with olives).
Moderate

In our restaurant recommendations, the first line indicates the arrondissement (district) and the closest métro stop.

Auberge Pyrénées-Cévennes

11th/Métro République
106 rue de la Folie-Méricourt (near blvd. Jules-Ferry)
Tel. 01/43.57.33.78
Closed Sat. (lunch) & Sun.
Small, charming restaurant serving the food of Southwest France.
Hams hanging from the ceiling add to the charm. Try the *cassoulet*.
Moderate - Expensive

L'Avant Goût

13th/Métro Place d'Italie
26 rue Bobillot
Tel. 01/53.80.24.00
Closed Sat., Sun., Mon. & most of Aug.
Mix with the French in this small, crowded bistro near the place
d'Italie. Consistently good cuisine and very French. Try the *pot-au-feu* (stew of meat and vegetables).
Moderate

Au Bascou

3rd/Métro Arts-et-Métiers
38 rue Réaumur (at rue Volta)
Tel. 01/42.72.69.25
Closed Sat., Sun. & part of Aug.
Modern bistro near the place de la République serving
Basque specialties, including *piperade* (a spicy omelet).
Moderate

Brioche.

Bistrot de L'Oulette (formerly Baracane)
4th/Métro Bastille
38 rue des Tournelles
Tel. 01/42.71.43.33
Closed Sat. (lunch) & Sun.
www.l-oulette.com
Small bistro in the Marais (near the place des Vosges) featuring the specialties of Southwest France (especially *confit*).
Moderate

Bistro des Deux Théâtres
9th/Métro Trinité
18 rue Blanche
Tel. 01/45.26.41.43
Open daily
www.bistrocie.fr
Affordable dining at this neighborhood bistro near the place de Clichy. Excellent *foie gras de canard* (fattened duck liver).
Moderate

Bistrot Paul-Bert
11th/Métro Faidherbe-Chaligny
18 rue Paul-Bert
Tel. 01/43.72.24.01
Closed Sun., Mon. & Aug.
A truly neighborhood bistro experience from its traditional decor to its menu written on a blackboard. Extensive wine list for such a small place. Try the *entrecôte* (rib-eye steak).
Moderate

Bouillon Racine
6th/Métro Cluny-La Sorbonne or Odéon
3 rue Racine
Tel. 01/44.32.15.60
Open daily
www.bouillon-racine.com
Popular brasserie in a historic building. Try the *waterzooi*. They also often offer a large vegetarian plate, and a huge beer selection.
Moderate

Bouillon Racine
Beautiful
Restaurant!

Bofinger
4th/Métro Bastille
5 rue de la Bastille
Tel. 01/42.72.87.82
Open daily until 1 a.m.
www.bofingerparis.com
Beautiful glass-roofed brasserie with lots of stained glass and brass,
located between the place des Vosges and the place de la Bastille. It's
the oldest Alsatian brasserie in Paris, and still serves traditional
dishes like *choucroute* (sauerkraut) and large platters of shellfish.
Moderate. (Across the street and less expensive is **Le Petit Bofinger**,
6 rue de la Bastille, Tel. 01/42.72.05.23.)

La Boulangerie
20th/Métro Ménilmontant
15 rue des Panoyaux (in the Ménilmontant area)
Tel. 01/43.58.45.45
Closed Sat. (lunch) & Sun.
Classic French bistro with a mosaic floor in a former bakery near
Père-Lachaise cemetery. Good selection of wines by the glass.
Moderate

Brasserie Balzar
5th/Métro Cluny-La Sorbonne
49 rue des Ecoles
Tel. 01/43.54.13.67
Open daily until midnight
www.brasseriebalzar.com
This Latin Quarter brasserie opened in 1898 and serves traditional
French cuisine. It's known for its *poulet rôti* (roast chicken), onion
soup and "colorful" waiters.
Moderate

Brasserie Flo
10th/Métro Château d'Eau
7 cour des Petites-Écuries (enter from 63 rue du Fg-St-Denis)
Tel. 01/47.70.13.59
Open daily until midnight
www.floparis.com

Alsatian food and Parisian atmosphere at this 1886 brasserie, on a passageway in an area not frequented by tourists. Jam-packed with some of the strangest people you'll see in Paris, and getting there is half the fun. Try the *gigot d'agneau* (leg of lamb).
Moderate

La Cave Gourmande
(Restaurant de Mark Singer)
19th/Métro Danube or Botzaris
10 rue du Général-Brunet
Tel. 01/40.40.03.30
Closed Sat., Sun. & part of Aug.

A bit out of the way but worth the trip.

Raves for the cuisine, but not for the trip out to this "remote" part of Paris. "Foodies" love this place, and we had one of our best meals here.
Moderate - Expensive

Chardenoux
11th/Métro Charonne
1 rue Jules-Vallès and 23 rue Chanzy
Tel. 01/43.71.49.52
Open daily
Traditional Parisian cooking in the Bastille/République. This small, friendly restaurant has been in business for almost 100 years. Try the duck terrine with figs.
Moderate

Chartier
9th/Métro Grands Boulevards
7 rue du Faubourg-Montmartre
Tel. 01/47.70.86.29
Open daily until 10 p.m.
No reservations
Traditional Paris soup kitchen. The *tripes à la mode de Caen* is a frequent special of the day (we passed on that). Lots of tourists, and you may be seated with strangers. Expect to wait in line.
Inexpensive

Chez Grisette
18th/Métro Abesses or Pigalle
14 rue Houdon
Tel. 01/42.62.04.80
Closed Sat., Sun. & Aug. No lunch
www.chez-grisette.fr
Delightful wine bar and bistro in the heart of Montmartre. A real
find. Start with the *terrine de campagne* (pork-and-liver *pâté*).
Inexpensive - Moderate

Chez Maître Paul
6th/Métro Odéon
12 rue Monsieur-le-Prince
Tel. 01/43.54.74.59
Closed Sun., Mon. (in July and Aug.) & part of Aug.
Hearty cooking of the Jura Mountains and Franche-Comté regions
of France (near the Swiss border), which are known for their game
and trout dishes.
Moderate

Chez Marianne
4th/Métro St-Paul
2 rue des Hospitalières-St-Gervais
Tel. 01/42.72.18.86
Open daily
No credit cards
Popular take-away deli (you can also eat here) known for its authen-
tic Jewish and Eastern European specialties, especially *falafel*.
Inexpensive

Chez Paul
11th/Métro Bastille or Ledru-Rollin
13 rue de Charonne (at rue de Lappe)
Tel. 01/47.00.34.57
Open daily
A favorite bistro in Paris. Never a bad meal, and ask to eat upstairs.
The service can be very Parisian, if you know what we mean. Try the
lapin (rabbit).
Moderate

La Closerie des Lilas

14th/Métro Raspail or Vavin
171 boulevard du Montparnasse
Tel. 01/40.51.34.50
Open daily
www.closeriedeslilas.fr
Lenin and Trotsky are among those who have visited this historic
café. There's a terrace, piano bar, brasserie (moderate) and
restaurant (expensive). The brasserie is known for its *steak tartare*
Moderate - Expensive

La Cordonnerie

1st/Métro Pyramides or Tuileries
20 rue St-Roch
Tel. 01/42.60.17.42
Closed Sat. & Sun.
Just behind the place Vendôme, this tiny, friendly family-run
restaurant serves classic French cuisine in a building dating back to
the 1640s.
Moderate

La Coupole

14th/Métro Vavin
102 boulevard du Montparnasse
Tel. 01/43.20.14.20
Open daily until 1 a.m.
www.lacoupoleparis.com
A Montparnasse institution since the days of Picasso, this noisy
brasserie known for its oysters is a favorite among tourists.
Moderate

Les Deux Musées

7th/Métro Solférino
5 rue de Bellechasse
Tel. 01/45.55.13.39
Closed Mon.
Try the delicious *poulet rôti* (roast chicken) at this unpretentious
restaurant just down the street from the Musée d'Orsay.
Moderate

Le Dix Vin
15th/Métro Pasteur
57 rue Falguière
Tel. 01/43.20.91.77
Closed Sat., Sun. & part of Aug.
No credit cards
www.le-dix-vins.com
Neighborhood wine bar in an area not frequented by many tourists
with traditional, reasonably priced Parisian bistro fare and wine
served by attentive waiters.
Moderate

L'Ecluse
8th/Métro Madeleine
15 place de la Madeleine (other locations throughout the city)
Tel. 01/42.65.34.69
Open daily
www.leclusebaravin.com
Chain of wine bars. Not the greatest food in Paris, but good for wine
tasting (especially Bordeaux). Decent selection of wines by the glass
and light meals such as *charcuterie assortie* (assorted cold meats).
Moderate

L'Enoteca
4th/Métro St-Paul
25 rue Charles V (at rue St-Paul)
Tel. 01/42.78.91.44
Closed part of Aug.
www.enoteca.fr
Attractive Italian wine bar/bistro in the Marais with one of the
largest Italian wine selections in Paris. Delicious *risotto*.
Moderate

La Fontaine de Mars
7th/Métro Ecole-Militaire
129 rue St-Dominique
Tel. 01/47.05.46.44
Open daily

One of our all-time favorites!

Red-checked tablecloths, friendly service and reasonable prices near the Eiffel Tower. Try the *poulet fermier aux morilles* (free-range chicken with morel mushrooms). Highly recommended.
Moderate

Le Fumoir
1st/Métro Louvre-Rivoli
6 rue de l'Amiral-de Coligny
Tel. 01/42.92.00.24
Open daily 11 a.m. to 2 a.m. Closed part of Aug.
www.lefumoir.com
This bar and restaurant is located near the Louvre. It's known for its Sunday brunch, salads, happy hour and *gâteau chocolat* (chocolate cake). There's a library in the back where you can have a drink and read (and exchange your own books for the ones in their library).
Inexpensive - Moderate

Au Gamin de Paris
4th/Métro St-Paul
51 rue Vieille du Temple
Tel. 01/42.78.97.24
Open daily
Small Marais bar/restaurant serving Parisian and Southwestern France specialties. Mostly meat dishes here. Fun crowd.
Moderate

Gaspard de la Nuit
4th/Métro Bastille
6 rue des Tournelles
Tel. 01/42.77.90.53
Open daily
www.legaspard.com
This cozy restaurant is located in the Marais between the place de la Bastille and place des Vosges. Traditional French cuisine. Try the delicious *carré d'agneau en croûte d'herbs* (loin of lamb with herbs).
Expensive

Gaya Rive Gauche
7th/Métro Rue du Bac
44 rue du Bac
Tel. 01/45.44.73.73
Closed Sat. (lunch), Sun. & Aug.
www.pierregagnaire.com
Chef Pierre Gagnaire has taken a fish house and converted it into a
sleek restaurant serving superb seafood.
Very Expensive

Le Grand Colbert
2nd/Métro Bourse
2 rue Vivienne (near the Place des Victoires)
Tel. 01/42.86.87.88
Closed part of Aug.
www.legrandcolbert.com
Housed in a restored historic building, serving traditional brasserie
cuisine. Known for its seafood tray. This stunning restaurant was
featured in the movie *Something's Gotta Give*.
Moderate

Le Hangar
3rd/Métro Rambuteau
12 impasse Berthaud (off of rue Beaubourg)
Tel. 01/42.74.55.44
Closed Sun., Mon. & Aug. No credit cards
Nothing fancy about this bistro near the Pompidou Center. Classic
French food at reasonable prices. Excellent *gâteau au chocolat*.
Inexpensive - Moderate

Il Cortile
1st/Métro Concorde or Madeleine
33/37 rue Cambon (in the Castille Hotel near the place Vendôme)
Tel. 01/44.58.44.58
Closed Sat., Sun. & Aug.
www.castille.com
Excellent Italian restaurant with an extensive wine list, attentive service and lovely outdoor terrace. Try the pappardelle with rabbit.
Expensive

These restaurants are very expensive and highly praised. Reservations well in advance are a must, as are jacket and tie.

Alain Ducasse
Restaurant Plaza Athénée
8th/Métro Alma-Marceau
25 avenue Montaigne
Tel. 01/53.67.65.00
www.alain-ducasse.com

L'Ambroisie
4th/Métro St-Paul
9 place des Vosges
Tel. 01/42.78.51.45

L'Arpège
7th/Métro Varenne
84 rue de Varenne
Tel. 01/47.05.09.06
www.alain-passard.com

L'Atelier de Joël Robuchon
7th/Métro Rue du Bac
5 rue de Montalembert
Tel. 01/42.22.56.56

Le Bristol
8th/Métro Miromesnil
112 rue du Faubourg St-Honoré
Tel. 01/53.43.43.00
www.lebristolparis.com

Le Cinq
8th/Métro George V
31 avenue George V (in the Four Seasons George V)
Tel. 01/49.52.71.54
www.fourseasons.com/paris

Le Grand Véfour
1st/Métro Palais-Royal
17 rue de Beaujolais
Tel. 01/42.96.56.27
www.relaischateaux.com/vefour

Guy Savoy
17th/Métro Charles-de-Gaulle-Étoile or Ternes
18 rue Troyon
Tel. 01/43.80.40.61
www.guysavoy.com

Jules Verne
7th/Métro Bir-Hakeim
Second level of the Eiffel Tower
Tel. 01/45.55.61.44
www.tour-eiffel.fr

Pierre Gagnaire
8th/Métro George V
6 rue Balzac (Hôtel Balzac)
Tel. 01/58.36.12.50
www.pierre-gagnaire.com

Senderens
8th/Métro Madeleine
9 place de la Madeleine
Tel. 01/42.65.22.90
www.senderens.fr

Taillevent
8th/Métro George V
15 rue Lamennais
Tel. 01/44.95.15.01
www.taillevent.com

La Tour d'Argent
5th/Métro Maubert-Mutualité
15-17 quai de la Tournelle
Tel. 01/43.54.23.31
www.latourdargent.com

Je Thé ... Me

15th/Métro Vaugirard

4 rue d'Alleray

Tel. 01/48.42.48.30

Closed Sun., Mon. & Aug.

The name is a play on Je t'aime... I Love you.

This attractive bistro in a century-old grocery store serves classic French fare. Very friendly.

Moderate

Juvenile's

1st/Métro Bourse

47 rue de Richelieu

Tel. 01/42.97.46.49

Closed Sun. & Mon (lunch)

This inexpensive, unpretentious wine bar serves light meals and has a large and interesting wine selection. Friendly and fun.

Inexpensive - Moderate

Ladurée

8th/Métro Madeleine

16 rue Royale

Tel. 01/42.60.21.79

Closed Sun. mid-July to mid-Aug.

www.laduree.fr

Pricey and elegant *salon de thé* and pastry shop. Also located at 8th/Métro George V, 75 avenue des Champs-Elysées 01/40.75.08.75.

Moderate - Expensive

Legrand Filles et Fils

2nd/Métro Bourse

1 rue de la Banque

Tel. 01/42.60.07.12

Open daily noon to 7 p.m.

www.caves-legrand.com

In the elegant Galerie Vivienne, this wine bar and shop has been run by the Legrand family for over three generations. Sandwiches, salads and cheese platters. A great place for a light lunch.

Moderate

Aux Lyonnais
2nd/Métro Bourse
32 rue St-Marc
Tel. 01/42.96.65.04
Closed Sat. (lunch), Sun. & Mon.
This beautiful century-old bistro has been recently renovated and
serves the cuisine of Lyon. The wine of choice is Beaujolais.
Moderate

Ma Bourgogne
4th/Métro St-Paul
19 place des Vosges
Tel. 01/42.78.44.64

*Ma Bourgogne
another favorite.*

Open daily. No credit cards
This café/restaurant in the place des Vosges (the oldest square in
Paris) serves traditional Parisian cuisine and specializes in *poulet rôti*
(roast chicken). Good salads.
Moderate

La Maison
5th/Métro St-Michel
1 rue de la Bûcherie
Tel. 01/43.29.73.57
Closed Mon. & Tue. (lunch)
An interesting crowd is found at this Latin Quarter bistro located
near the Seine. In good weather, the tables on the small square in
front of the restaurant are a great place to dine. Try the *epaule
d'agneau de sept heures* (shoulder of lamb cooked for seven hours).
Moderate

Mariage-Frères
6th/Métro Odéon or Saint-Michel
13 rue des Grands Augustins
Tel. 01/40.51.82.50
Open daily
400 types of teas served in elegant salons serving light meals and
weekend brunch. Also at 4th/Métro Hôtel de Ville, 30-32 rue du
Bourg-Tibourg, Tel. 01/42.72.28.11 and 8th/Métro Ternes, 260 rue
du Faubourg Saint-Honoré, Tel. 01/46.22.18.54.
Moderate

Muscade

1st/Métro Palais Royal

36 rue de Montpensier (within the Palais Royal gardens)

Tel. 01/42.97.51.36

Closed Mon.

www.muscade-palais-royal.com

A delightful place for lunch especially in nice weather when you can sit amid the lovely gardens. This little restaurant/tearoom is a perfect place to come when visiting the nearby Louvre. Great salads and delicious homemade desserts. Dinner served from May to August.

Moderate

Nicolas

8th/Métro Madeleine

31 Place de la Madeleine

Tel. 01/42.68.00.16/01.49.24.08.52

Great place for a cheap lunch.

Open 9:30 a.m. to 8:00 p.m. Closed Sun.

Located upstairs from the Nicolas wine shop. You can buy a bottle of wine at the shop and have it served with your meal. The menu is limited, but the wines sold by the glass are inexpensive.

Moderate

Oudino

7th/Métro Vaneau

17 rue Oudino

Tel. 01/45.66.05.09

Closed Sat. (lunch) & Sun.

www.oudino.com

This newcomer to our book is located on an attractive small street. You can start your meal with a *salade caesar* (Caesar salad) and dine on excellent *entrecôte* served with a *béarnaise* sauce. A real find.

Moderate

Les Papilles

5th/Métro Cluny-La Sorbonne (or RER Luxembourg)

30 rue Gay-Lussac

Tel. 01/43.25.20.79

Closed Sun. & part of Aug.

Near the Panthéon, *Les Papilles* (Tastebuds) sells gourmet foods and wine, and offers creative takes on French cuisine. Try the tender hanger steak. Worth the trip!
Moderate

Perraudin
5th/Métro Cluny-La Sorbonne
157 rue Saint-Jacques
Tel. 01/46.33.15.75
No reservations. No credit cards
Open daily until 10:30 p.m.
www.restaurantperraudin.com
You'll get to know your fellow diners at this inexpensive bistro serving traditional Parisian cuisine just steps from the Panthéon.
Inexpensive - Moderate

Le Petit Marguery
13th/Métro Les Gobelins
9 boulevard de Port-Royal
Tel. 01/43.31.58.59
Closed Sun., Mon. & Aug.
www.petitmarguery.fr
This 1930s bistro features game dishes and is known for its Grand Marnier *soufflé* and good service.
Moderate

Au Petit Riche
9th/Métro Le Peletier or Richelieu-Drouot
25 rue Le Peletier (at rue Rossini)
Tel. 01/47.70.68.68
Closed Sun.
www.aupetitriche.com
This classic bistro serves specialties of the Loire Valley with a Parisian twist. Try the *civet* (game stew).
Moderate

Polidor

6th/Métro Odéon
41 rue Monsieur-le-Prince
Tel. 01/43.26.95.34
Open daily
No reservations. No credit cards
Popular old-fashioned bistro serving traditional cuisine such as
pintade (guinea hen).
Inexpensive

Le Procope

6th/Métro Odéon
13 rue de l'Ancienne Comédie
Tel. 01/40.46.79.00
Open daily until midnight
www.procope.com
The oldest brasserie in Paris. Benjamin Franklin is said to have dined
here. Traditional French cuisine served in small dining rooms. Very
touristy. Take a stroll down the cour du Commerce, a charming alley
behind Le Procope.
Moderate

Le Reminet

5th/Métro Maubert-Mutualité or St-Michel
5 rue des Grands-Degrés
Tel. 01/44.07.04.24
Closed Tue., Wed. & part of Aug.
Small Latin Quarter bistro with modern French cooking, attentive
service, and outdoor seating in the summer. Try the grilled lamb
when available.
Moderate

Restaurant de la Tour

15th/Métro Dupleix
6 rue Desaix
Tel. 01/43.06.04.24
Closed Sun. and Mon.
www.restaurant-latour.fr

You'll be welcomed by the friendly owners to the lovely dining room with Provençal décor where you'll dine on classic French fare. Try the delicious *sanglier* (wild boar). After dinner, head to the brilliantly lit Eiffel Tower, just a few blocks away.

Moderate

Restaurant du Musée d'Orsay

7th/Métro Solférino
1 rue Légion d'Honneur/162 rue de Lille
Tel. 01/45.49.47.03
Lunch 11:45 a.m. to 2:45 p.m. Dinner Thu. only 7 p.m. to 9:30 p.m.
Closed Mon.
www.musee-orsay.fr
This restaurant is located in the beautiful Musée d'Orsay (a former rail station) and serves a reasonably priced buffet lunch in an ornate dining room. Not bad for a museum restaurant.

Moderate

Roger La Grenouille

6th/Métro Odéon
26 rue des Grands Augustins
Tel. 01/56.24.24.34
Closed Sun.
This quirky restaurant (it seems that everyone is having fun and the service is friendly) was founded in 1930 and serves good food at moderate prices. Especially good are the *coq au vin* and the *tournedos Rossini*. If you've had enough to drink, you may find yourself wearing one of the silly hats scattered throughout the restaurant.

Moderate

La Rôtisserie d'en Face

6th/Métro Odéon or St-Michel
2 rue Christine
Tel. 01/43.26.40.98
Closed Sat. (lunch) and Sun.
www.jacques-cagna.com

Modern rotisserie in the St-Germain area known for its imaginative, grilled dishes. Try the *côtelettes d'agneau grillées* (grilled lamb chops).

Moderate

7ème Sud Grenelle

7th/Métro La Tour-Maubourg
159 rue de Grenelle
Tel. 01/44.18.30.30
Open daily

The odd name means that this restaurant is in the 7th arrondissement at the south end of rue Grenelle. This small, modern restaurant serves French, Mediterranean (lots of pasta dishes) and North African (try the *tagine*) cuisine. Friendly service.
Moderate

Le Severo

14th/Métro Alésia or Mouton-Duvernet
8 rue des Plantes
Tel. 01/45.40.40.91
Closed Sat., Sun. and Aug.

Another favorite.

Small bistro away from the tourists. The chef used to be a butcher and the beef here is fantastic. I'd make the trip just for the fries! The wine blackboard fills a whole wall of this bistro. Looking for a truly Parisian experience? This is the place.
Moderate

Sorza

4th/Métro Pont-Marie
51 rue Saint-Louis-en-I'lle (on the Île St-Louis)
Tel. 01/43.54.78.62
Open daily
www.restaurant-sorza.fr

This small, modern Italian restaurant with stark red-and-black decor is a newcomer on the lovely Île St-Louis. Try the *filet de volaille aux morilles et fetuccine* (chicken fillet with morels & fetuccine) and end with the sinfully rich *mousse au chocolat* (chocolate mousse).
Moderate-Expensive

Le Souk

11th/Métro Bastille
1 rue Keller
Tel. 01/49.29.05.08
Closed Mon. No lunch Tue. - Fri.

This popular Moroccan restaurant with a good selection of vegetarian dishes is always busy and the interior is exotic.
Moderate

Spicy

8th/Métro F.D.-Roosevelt
8 ave. F.D.-Roosevelt (near the Champs-Élysées)
Tel. 01/56.59.62.59
Open daily for lunch and dinner
www.spicyrestaurant.com
Modern French cuisine is served by a friendly, English-speaking staff to an international clientele. The roast chicken is a good choice. Excellent desserts (try the chocolate cake). The house red Bordeaux is a good value at about 20 euros per bottle. The only thing "wrong" with this restaurant is its name, as the food isn't particularly spicy.
Moderate-Expensive

Terminus Nord

10th/Métro Gare du Nord
23 rue de Dunkerque
Tel. 01/42.85.05.15
Open daily until 1 a.m.
www.terminusnord.com
What a great way to arrive in (or depart from) Paris! This large, bustling brasserie near the Gare du Nord is just so Parisian with its mahogany bar, polished wood and beveled glass. Seafood platters, *bouillabaisse* and duck breast are the featured dishes.
Moderate

Le Timbre

6th/Métro Notre-Dame-des-Champs
3 rue Ste-Beuve (off of rue Notre-Dame-des-Champs)
Closed Sun., Mon. (lunch) & part of Aug.
Tel. 01/45.49.10.40
The name means "stamp" which is appropriate for this tiny Left Bank bistro. A wonderful Parisian experience. How does the English chef turn out such wonderful dishes in such a small kitchen?
Inexpensive - Moderate

Aux Trois Petits Cochons
2nd/Métro Etienne Marcel
31 rue Tiquetonne
Tel. 01/42.33.39.69
Open daily. No lunch
www.auxtroispetitscochons.fr
Lively, friendly and gay (in every sense of the word) bistro in the
Montorgueil quarter. Excellent *blanquette de veau* (veal stew).
Moderate

Le Train Bleu
12th/Métro Gare-de-Lyon
20 boulevard Diderot (in the Gare de Lyon train station)
Tel. 01/44.75.76.76
Open daily until 11 p.m.
www.le-train-bleu.com
Forget all the food you've eaten in train stations. It's delicious here.
The setting, with its murals of the French-speaking world, is spectac-
ular. A great place to have a drink.
Expensive

Vin Sur Vin
7th/Métro Alma Marceau
20 rue de Monttessuy
Tel. 01/47.05.14.20
Closed Sat. (lunch), Sun. & Mon (lunch)
Great wine and creative cuisine near the Eiffel Tower. Try the pan-
seared *rouget* (red mullet) or farm-raised pigeon. End your meal
with delicious *mille-feuille* (light pastry w/cream filling).
Moderate - Expensive

Willi's Wine Bar
1st/Métro Bourse
13 rue des Petits-Champs
Tel. 01/42.61.05.09 (www.williswinebar.com)
Closed Sun. and part of Aug.
British owners serving specialties with Mediterranean influences. A
great wine list, and a favorite of many travelers to Paris.
Moderate

Wine bars are listed above in the *Places to Eat* section of this guide.

Au Lapin Agile
18th/Métro Lamarck-Caulaincourt
22 rue des Saules (at rue St-Vincent)
Tel. 01/46.06.85.87
Open Tue. to Sun. 9 p.m. to 2 a.m.
www.au-lapin-agile.com
You sit at small wooden tables and listen to French folk tunes at this
shuttered cottage once frequented by Picasso. Cover charge is 24
euros and includes one drink.

Buddha Bar
8th/Métro Concorde
8 rue Boissy d'Anglais
Tel. 01/53.05.90.00
Open daily. No lunch on Sat. and Sun.
www.buddah-bar.com
Asian-themed, trendy bar known for its music. Expensive cocktails,
and can be a little touristy at times.

Le Dokhan
16th/Métro Trocadéro
117 rue Lauriston (in Trocadéro Dokhan's Hôtel)
Tel. 01/53.65.66.99
Open daily 11 a.m. to 2 a.m.
An elegant champagne bar where you
can enjoy it by the flute or by the bottle.

Coupe de Champagne.

Le Trésor
4th/Métro Hôtel de Ville or St-Paul
5-7 rue du Trésor (off of rue Vieille du Temple)
Tel. 01/42.71.35.17
Open Mon. to Fri. 5 p.m. to 2 a.m., Sat. & Sun. noon to 2 a.m.
Cocktails served both inside and outside at tables along this lovely,
flowered street in the heart of the Marais. Great people-watching.

Bakeries (Boulangeries), Chocolate Shops (Chocolateries), Pastry Shops (Pâtisseries) and Candy Stores (Confiseries)

Kayser
5th/Métro Maubert-Mutualité
8 and 14 rue Monge
Tel. 01/44.07.01.42 and 01/44.07.17.81
Closed Tue.
Excellent *baguettes*, specialty breads like the coarse and hearty *pain au levain*, and delicious *pain au chocolate*.

Lenôtre
8th/Métro Champs-Elysées – Clemenceau
10 avenue des Champs-Elysées
Tel. 01/42.65.85.10
Closed part of Aug.
www.lenotre.fr
Café, kitchen shop (everything from pots and pans to wine) and cooking school all in the elegant glass-and-stone Pavillon Elysée. Lenôtre has eleven other shops in Paris.

La Maison du Chocolat
8th/Métro Ternes
225 rue du Faubourg-St-Honoré
Tel. 01/42.27.39.44
Closed Sun.
Every chocolate lover should visit. There are also shops at:
52 rue François 1er (8th/Métro Franklin-D.-Roosevelt),
8 boulevard de la Madeleine (9th/Métro Madeleine),
19 rue de Sèvres (6th/Métro Sèvres Babylone), Printemps (2nd floor)), 64 blvd. Hausmann (9th/Métro Havre-Caumartin), and Carrousel du Louvre, 99 rue de Rivoli (1st/Métro Palais Royal).

Marquise de Sévigné

The marquise de Sévigné lived in what is now the Carnavalet Museum.

8th/Métro Madeleine
32 place de la Madeleine
Tel. 01/42.65.19.47
Closed Sun.
A French "luxury" (their word) chocolate maker since 1898.

Patrick Roger
6th/Métro Odéon
108 boulevard St-Germain-des-Prés
Tel. 01/43.29.38.42
Closed Sun. & Mon.
Patrick Roger's friendly shop on the boulevard St-Germain-des-Prés
has excellent chocolates packaged in green boxes that make great
gifts and are easy to pack to take home. Also at 45 avenue Victor
Hugo (16th/Métro Kleber).

Stohrer
2nd/Métro Les Halles
51 rue Montorgueil
Tel. 01/42.33.38.20
Closed part of Aug.
The Parisian favorite of *baba au rhum* (spongecake soaked in rum)
was invented at this *pâtisserie* in the Montorgueil quarter.

A La Mère de Famille
9th/Métro Le Peletier or Cadet
35 rue du Faubourg-Montmartre
Tel. 01/47.70.83.69
Closed Sun., Mon. & Aug.
The oldest *confiserie* in Paris (since 1761).

A L'Etoile d'Or
9th/Métro Pigalle
30 rue Fontaine
Tel. 01/48.74.59.55
Closed Sun. & most Mon.
This incredible store, near the tacky sex shops of the Pigalle area,
has some of the best candy concoctions you could ever imagine.

Alléosse

17th/Métro Ternes
13 rue Poncelet
Tel. 01/46.22.50.45
Closed Sun. (afternoon) & Mon.

Cheese is like gold to the French. Charles de Gaulle is reported to have said, "How can anyone govern a nation that has 246 different kinds of cheese?" This pretty cheese shop on a busy market street serves rare cheeses from throughout France.

Barthélemy

7th/Métro Rue du Bac
51 rue de Grenelle
Tel. 01/45.48.56.75
Closed Sun., Mon. & Aug.

This small cheese shop on the Left Bank is where Parisians shop for their cheese. When you walk in, you're overtaken by the intense smell of some of the best cheese available in France.

Specialty Food Stores (Épiceries)

Albert Ménès

8th/Métro Madeleine or St-Augustin
41 boulevard Malesherbes
Tel. 01/42.66.95.63
Closed Sat., Sun. & mid-July to mid-Aug.

Gourmet food shop that specializes in food from the provinces.

Boutique Maille

8th/Métro Madeleine
6 place de la Madeleine
Tel. 01/40.15.06.00
Closed Sun.
Boutique mustard shop on the
place de la Madeleine.

Caviar Kaspia
8th/Métro Madeleine
17 place de la Madeleine
Tel. 01/42.65.33.32 (restaurant)/Tel. 01/42.65.66.21 (store)
Closed Sun.
Caviar, blinis and salmon. There's also a restaurant upstairs.

Fauchon
8th/Métro Madeleine
26 place de la Madeleine
Tel. 01/70.39.38.00
Closed Sun.

Do not touch the food! A clerk must get it for you.

Deli and grocery known for its huge selection of canned food, baked goods and alcohol. The store is a must for those wanting to bring back French specialties.

Gourmet Lafayette
8th/Métro Chaussée-d'Antin
40 boulevard Hausmann (in the Galeries Lafayette department store)
Tel. 01/42.82.34.56
Closed Sun.
This department store has a huge gourmet-food section.

La Grande Épicerie
7th/Métro Sèvres Babylone
38 rue Sèvres (in Au Bon Marché department store)
Tel. 01/44.39.81.00
Closed Sun.
The *ultimate* grocery store (with wine cellar and carry-out). Don't miss it!

Hédiard
8th/Métro Madeleine
21 place de la Madeleine
Tel. 01/43.12.88.88
Closed Sun.
Food store/spice shop that has been open since the 1850s, similar to Fauchon, with an on-site restaurant.

La Maison du Miel
9th/Métro Madeleine or Opéra
24 rue Vignon
Tel. 01/47.42.26.70
Open daily
This food store located around the corner from Fauchon offers everything made from honey (from sweets to soap).

Oliviers & Co.
Olive oils from around the Mediterranean at several lovely shops: 2nd/90 rue Montorgueil, 4th/47 rue Vieille du Temple, 4th/81 rue St Louis en l'Ile, 5th/128 rue Mouffetard, 6th/28 rue de Buci, 7th/44 rue Cler, 12th/Bercy Village, 15th/85 rue du Commerce, and 17th/8 bis rue de Lévis.
www.oliviers-co.com

Wine Stores (Caves), Wine Tastings, and Cooking Schools

Les Caves Augé
8th/Métro Saint-Augustin
116 boulevard Haussmann
Tel. 01/45.22.16.97
Closed Sun. & Mon. (morning)
Famous wine shop since 1850 offering everything from prestige wines to foreign vintages.

Lavinia
1st/Métro Madeleine
3-5 boulevard de la Madeleine
Tel. 01/42.97.20.20
Closed Sun. Open until 8:00 p.m.
The largest wine shop in Paris with 2000 foreign wines, 3000 French wines and 1000 spirits, priced from 3 to 3600 euros. Drink any bottle from the shop at the wine bar. Lunch served (with wine, of course). No dinner.

Ô Chateau

11th/Métro République
100 rue de la Folie Méricourt
Tel. 01/44.73.97.80/www.o-chateau.com (reservations)
"Coming to Paris and not tasting good French wines is like going to the U.S. and not trying a good burger," says Olivier Magny. This young French sommelier will guide you through a fun, informative and relaxing wine tasting in his Parisian loft. From 20 euros.

Les Caves Taillevent

8th/Métro Charles-de-Gaulle-Étoile or Saint-Philippe-du-Roule
199 rue du Faubourg-Saint-Honoré
Tel. 01/45.61.14.09/www.taillevent.com
Open 10 a.m. to 7:30 p.m.. Closed Sun. & Aug.
This wine shop is associated with the well-known Taillevent restaurant and is said to have over 500,000 bottles of wine starting at around 5 euros. You'll be amazed at the cost of some selections.

La Dernière Goutte

6th/Métro St-Germain-des-Prés
6 rue de Bourbon-le-Château   *The last drop.*
Tel. 01/43.29.11.62
Closed Mon. (morning)
Located in an old vaulted room. The owners are charming and friendly, and they generally have wine tastings.

Nicolas

Over 200 wine stores located throughout Paris. The main one is in the 8th/Métro Madeleine at 31 place de la Madeleine. Tel. 01/42.68.00.16. Closed Sun. www.nicolas-wines.com

L'Atelier des Chefs

8th/Métro Miromesnil
10 rue de Penthièvre
Tel. 01/53.30.05.82 (reservations)
www.atelierdeschefs.com

Why not dine at a prestigious cooking school? Half-hour cooking class (in French, but all you have to do is follow along) with lunch. From 15 euros.

Café Beaubourg
4th/Métro Rambuteau
100 rue Saint-Martin
Tel. 01/48.87.63.96
Open daily 8 a.m. to 1 p.m. (Sat. & Sun. until 2 a.m.)
Looking onto the Centre Pompidou and packed with an artsy crowd.
The bathrooms are worth the trip.

Café de Flore
6th/Métro Saint-Germain-des-Prés
172 boulevard. Saint-Germain-des-Prés
Tel. 01/45.48.55.26
Open daily 7:30 a.m. to 1:30 a.m.
www.cafe-de-flore.com
Another famous café and a favorite of tourists and Parisians alike
(next door to Les Deux Magots).

Café de la Paix
9th/Métro Opéra
12 boulevard des Capucines (place de l'Opéra)
Tel. 01/40.07.36.36
Open daily 7 a.m. to midnight
www.cafedelapaix.fr
Famous café (not really known for its food). Popular with tourists.
Another spot for outdoor people-watching
(and the inside is stunnning).

Café de l'Industrie
11th/Métro Bastille
16-17 rue St-Sabin
Tel. 01/47.00.13.53
Open daily 10 a.m. to 2 a.m.
Near the Opéra Bastille, this inexpensive
café features a limited menu, a diverse wine
list, and an interesting crowd.

Café Les Deux Magots

6th/Métro Saint-Germain-des-Prés
6 place Saint-Germain-des-Prés
Tel. 01/45.48.55.25
Open daily 7:30 a.m. to 1 a.m.
www.cafelesdeuxmagots.com
If you're a tourist, you'll fit right in at one of Hemingway's favorite spots. We don't really recommend that you eat here (there is a limited menu), but have a drink and enjoy the great people-watching.

Café L'Été en Pente Douce

L'été en pente douce ~ Summer on a gentle slope.

18th/Métro Château-Rouge
23 rue Muller
Tel. 01/42.64.02.67
Open daily noon to 3 p.m. and 7 p.m. to midnight
Interesting and picturesque Montmartre café near Sacré-Coeur. Take a break here after you climb the steps to Sacré-Coeur!

Café Marly

1st/Métro Musée du Louvre/Palais-Royal
93 rue de Rivoli
Tel. 01/49.26.06.60
Open daily 8 a.m. to 2 a.m.
This café overlooks the pyramid
at the Louvre and no place in
Paris has a better setting. Standard
bistro fare served by waiters in suits.

we LOVE the pyramids.

It's a great place for a relaxing lunch or, come here after dinner and end your day with a glass of champagne. Definitely worth the cost!

Pause Café

11th/Métro Ledru-Rollin
41 rue de Charonne
Tel. 01/48.06.80.33
Open daily 8 a.m. to 1 a.m.
Popular café specializing in
tourtes.

If you're looking for a comprehensive guide to speaking French, this is not the right place. What follows are simply a few tips for speaking French and a very brief pronunciation guide.

It is always good to learn a few polite terms so that you can excuse yourself when you've stepped on the foot of an elderly lady or spilled your drink down the back of the gentleman in front of you. It's also just common courtesy to greet the people you meet in your hotel, in shops and restaurants in their own language.

If a word ends in a consonant and that word is followed by a word that starts in a vowel, the consonant is linked to the vowel. So, **vous avez** (you have) is pronounced voozavay. And the final consonant in a word is silent (unless followed by an e).

a like in far
e like in open
é and ez like the a in rate
è like the e in bet
ê like eh as in *crêpe*
i like the i in machine
o like the o in not
ô like the o in wrote
u round your lips as to say oh, but say ee
an, am, en, em, ant, ent like the a in wand
au, eau like the o in okay
er at the end of a word sounds like the ay in day
in, im, ain, aim like the a in sank
ou like the oo in cool
oi like the wa in water
que like the cu in curve
qui like kee

un is pronounced uhn
c like a k before a, o, u and consonants
c like an s before e and i
ch like sh
ç like the s in simple
g before a, o and u like in good
g like the s in pleasure before i and e
gn like the ny in canyon
h is always silent
j like the s in measure
r like an r being swallowed
s like the s in step but when between vowels, it's pronounced like a z
ss like an s
zh like the s in measure

This is a brief listing of some familiar English foods and food-related words that you may need in a restaurant setting. It is followed by a list of phrases that may come in handy. There are also some pronunciation prompts. They aren't all exactly right, but they're close enough to get you what you need.

allergic, allergique
anchovies, anchois *anchois~ an-shwa*
appetizer, hors-d'oeuvre
apple, pomme
artichoke, artichaut
ashtray, cendrier
asparagus, asperge
bacon, lard (lardons)
baked, au four/cuit au four
banana, banane
beans, fève
beef, boeuf
beefsteak, bifteck/steak
beer, bière
beverages, boissons
bill, l'addition
bitter, amer
boiled, bouilli
bottle (half), demi-bouteille
bottle, bouteille *boutielle~ boo-tay*
bowl, bol
braised, braisé
bread, pain
bread roll, petit pain

breakfast, petit déjeuner
broth, consommé
butter, beurre
cabbage, chou
cake, gâteau
candle, chandelle/bougie
carrot, carotte
cereal, céréale(s)
chair, chaise
check, chèque
cheers, santé
cheese, fromage
cherry, cerise
chicken, poulet
chicken breast, suprême de volaille
chops, côtelettes, côtes
clams, palourdes
cocktail, cocktail
cod, morue
coffee, café
coffee (American-style), café américain
coffee w/milk, café crème/un crème (*café au lait* if you want a lot of milk)
coffee (black), café noir
coffee (decaf), déca/décafféiné
cold, froid
corn, maïs
cover charge, couvert
credit card, carte de crédit
cucumber, concombre
cup, tasse
custard, crème anglaise
dessert, dessert
dinner, dîner

dish (plate), assiette. A main dish is *plat principal*

drink, boisson

duck, canard

eggs, oeufs

espresso, café express/un express

fish, poisson

fish soup, bouillabaisse (the famous seafood stew)

fork, fourchette

french fries, frites (pommes frites)

fresh, fraîche/frais

fried, frit

fruit, fruits

game, gibier

garlic, ail *ail ~ aye*

gin, gin

glass, verre

goat, chèvre

goose, oie

grapefruit, pamplemousse

grapes, raisin

green beans, haricots verts

grilled, grillé

ham (cooked), jambon (cuit)

ham (cured), jambon (de Parme & de Bayonne)

hamburger, hamburger

honey, miel

hot, chaud *Chaud ~ Froid*

ice, glaçon *SHOW ~*

ice cream, glace *FWA*

ice (on the rocks), avec des glaçons

ice water, l'eau glacée

included, compris

ketchup, ketchup

knife, couteau *Couteau - coo.to*

kosher, casher/kascher

lamb, agneau

large, grand

lemon, citron

lettuce, laitue

little, petit/peu de...

liver, foie

lobster, homard

loin, longe (pork)/aloyau (beef)

lunch, déjeuner *déjeuner ~*

match, allumette *day- juh-n*

mayonnaise, mayonnaise

meat, viande

medium (cooked), à point

melon, melon

menu, carte

milk, lait

    Lait écrémé is skim milk

    & *lait entier*, whole milk

mineral water, eau minérale

mineral water (sparkling), eau minérale (gazeuse)

mineral water (w/out carbonation), eau minérale plate (non gazeuse)

mixed, mélange, mixte, mesclun (salad greens)

mushrooms, champignons

mussels, moules

mustard, moutarde

napkin, serviette

noodles, pâtes/nouilles

nuts, noix

octopus, poulpes

oil, huile
olive oil, huile d'olive
olives, olives
omelette, omelette
on the rocks (w/ ice), avec des glaçons
onions, oignons *oignons ~*
orange, orange *ON-yone*
orange juice, jus d'orange
overdone, trop cuit *huîtres ~*
oysters, huîtres *weeT-RAH*
partridge, perdrix
pastry, pâtisserie
peaches, pêches
pears, poires
peas, petits pois
pepper (black), poivre
peppers (sweet), poivrons
perch, perche
pineapple, ananas
plate (dish), assiette
please, s'il vous plaît
plums, prunes
poached, poché
pork, porc
potatoes, pommes de terre
poultry, volaille
prawns, grosses crevettes/ langoustines
quail, caille
rabbit, lapin
rare, saignant
raspberry, framboises
receipt, note/reçu
rice, riz
roast, rôti
rolls, petits pains

salad, salade
salmon, saumon
salt, sel
sandwich, sandwich(e)
sauce, sauce
sautéed, sauté
scallops, coquilles (Saint-Jacques) *brouille ~*
scrambled, brouillé *brew-ee*
seafood, fruits de mer
seasonings, condiments/ assaisonnement
shellfish, crustacés
shrimp, crevettes
small, petit
smoked, fumé
snails, escargots
sole, sole
soup, soupe
spaghetti, spaghetti
sparkling (wine), champagne
specialty, spécialité *epicé ~*
spicy, épicé *AY-PEE-SAY*
spinach, épinards
spoon, cuiller/cuillère
squid, calmar/calamar
steak, steak/bifteck
steamed, vapeur
stew, ragoût
strawberries, fraises
sugar, sucre
sugar substitute, édulcorant/de l'aspartam
supper, dîner
sweet, doux/sucré
table, table
tea, thé

tea w/lemon, thé citron

tea w/milk, thé au lait

thank you, merci

tip, pourboire

toast, pain grillé *grillé ~ gree-AY*

tomato, tomate

toothpick, cure-dents

trout, truite

tuna, thon

turkey, dindon/dinde

utensil, couvert

veal, veau

vegetable, légume

vegetarian, végétarien

venison, venaison

vinegar, vinaigre

vodka, vodka

waiter, monsieur (never *garçon*)

waitress, madame or mademoiselle

water, eau

watermelon, pastèque

well done, bien cuit. Very well done is *très bien cuit*

whipped cream, crème chantilly *(shan-tee-ee)*

wine, vin

wine list, carte des vins

wine (red), vin rouge

wine (rosé), vin rosé

wine (white), vin blanc

with, avec

without, sans

yogurt, yaourt

Helpful phrases

please, s'il vous plaît

thank you, merci

yes, oui

no, non

good morning, bonjour

good afternoon, bonjour

good evening, bonsoir

good night, bonne nuit

goodbye, au revoir

Do you speak English?, parlez-vous anglais?

I don't speak French, je ne parle pas français

excuse me, pardon

I don't understand, je ne comprends pas

I'd like a table, je voudrais une table

I'd like to reserve a table, je voudrais réserver une table

for one person, pour une personne *-UNE*

for two, pour deux *- deh*

--trois (3) *-Twa*

--quatre (4) *- CaT*

--cinq (5) *- Sank*

--six (6) *- see*

--sept (7) *- seT*

--huit (8) *- weeT*

--neuf (9) *- nurf*

--dix (10) *- deece*

this evening, ce soir

tomorrow, demain

near the window, près de la fenêtre

with a view, avec vue

outside on the patio, sur la terrasse

no smoking, non-fumeur. As of January 2008, smoking is banned in all restaurants

where is?, où est

where are?, où sont

the bathrooms, les toilettes

the bill, l'addition

a mistake (error), une erreur

Is service included?, Le service est-il compris?

Do you accept credit cards?, acceptez-vous les cartes de crédit

traveler's checks, chèques de voyage

How much is it?, c'est combien?

What is this?, qu'est-ce que c'est?

I did not order this, ce n'est pas ce que j'ai commandé

This is, c'est

--too, trop *— Trow*

--cold, froid *— FWA*

--hot, chaud *— SHow*

--not fresh, n'est pas frais *— NAY PAH FRAIS*

--rare, saignant *— SANE-YANT*

--undercooked, pas assez cuit *— PAH AHSAY CWEE*

--overcooked, trop cuit *TROW CWEE*

--delicious, délicieux

I am a vegeterian, Je suis végétarien(ne)

without meat, pas de viande/sans viande

closed, fermé

Monday, lundi *Lundee .*

Tuesday, mardi *Mardee*

Wednesday, mercredi *Mare KRAdee*

Thursday, jeudi *Juh dee*

Friday, vendredi *Vawndradee*

Saturday, samedi *Samahdee*

Sunday, dimanche *Dee mansh*

AAAAA, the seal of approval of
*l'Association Amicale des Amateurs
d'Andouillettes Authentiques.*
Only in France would they have an
association for devotees of
andouillette (tripe sausage)

*In French
Amateur mean.
"Lover of"*

abats, abattis, organ meats

abricot, apricot

acras/accras, *beignets,* usually stuffed
w/seafood, found in the French West Indies

acidulé, acidic

addition (l'addition), check/bill

affinée, aged

agneau, lamb

agneau de lait, milk-fed lamb

agneau pré-salé, lamb grazed on salt marshes

agrumes, citrus fruits   *Agrumes.*

aiglefin, haddock

aïgo bouido, garlic soup (means "boiled water")

aigre, sour

aigre-doux, sweet & sour

aigrelette, a sour sauce

aiguebelle, herbal after-dinner drink similar to *Chartreuse*

aiguillette, thin slice. *Aiguillette de boeuf* are slices of steak

ail, garlic

aile, wing of poultry

*Aile is used
to mean
white meat.*

aile de raie, ray fin (a kite-shaped
fish also called skate)

aile et cuisse, *aile*: literally wing,
it means white meat in fowl
cuisse: literally leg, it means dark meat in fowl

ailerons, wings

aillade, garlic mayonnaise (see *aïoli*)

aillade gasconne, veal w/garlic found in Southwest France

aïoli/ailloli, garlic mayonnaise. Found in many
provençal dishes

aïoli garni, *aïoli* served w/boiled food, salt cod, vegetables & eggs

airelle, cranberry

à la, à l', au, aux, in the manner of, in, with

à la carte, side dishes (each item ordered separately)

albert, a sauce of egg yolk, cream, horseradish, shallots & mustard

albuféra, *béchamel* sauce w/sweet peppers

alcool, alcohol

algues, seaweed

ali baba, spongecake soaked in rum

aligot, garlic mashed potatoes w/cheese

alimentation, food/food store

allumettes, puff pastry or potato strips

alose, shad (fish)

alouette, lark

alouette sans tête, rolled veal slice
    stuffed w/garlic & minced meat

*Alouettes
Sans têtes ~
Larks
without
heads!*

aloyau, sirloin

Alsace, located in the northeast corner of France (along the
    German border); one of France's wine regions specializing
    in white wines such as Gewürztraminer, Riesling, Pinot Gris,
    Pinot Blanc, Pinot Noir & Sylvaner

alsacienne, alsacien/usually garnished w/sausage & sauerkraut
    (means "Alsace style")

amande, almond

amande de mer, small shellfish

amandine, w/almonds

amer/amère, bitter

américaine, white wine sauce usually w/brandy,
    shallots, tomatoes & garlic w/shrimp/lobster

Amer Picon, aperitif (wine & brandy w/herbs)

amidon, starch. *Amidon de blé* is cornstarch

amourettes, the bone marrow of an ox or calf

amuse-bouche, appetizer

amuse-gueule, appetizer

ananas, pineapple

anchoïade, anchovy spread from Provence

anchois, anchovy

ancienne, "old style": usually means a
    wine cream sauce w/mushrooms,
    shallots or onions

*Bouche ~ mouth
gueule ~ throat
These are small
morsels of food
Just a mouthful
or two.*

andalouse, usually w/eggplant, tomatoes
    & green peppers

andouille, tripe sausage

andouillette, small tripe sausage

aneth, dill

angélique, the crystallized stalks of
the herb angelica
(a decoration for cakes)

anglaise, boiled/boiled or steamed
vegetables/breaded, fried meat,
fish or vegetables

We have a general rule about tripe: Don't. But we love andouillette.

anguille, eel. Many dishes in the French West Indies feature eels

anguille au vert, eel in a white sauce w/parsley

anis, aniseed

apéritif, drink before dinner

à point, medium rare

appellation d'origine contrôlée, an officially recognized wine
of France. Sometimes designated by A.O.C. The makers of
A.O.C. are the best of the French wine industry

arachide, peanut

araignée de mer, spider crab

ardennaise, usually means served w/berries ("Ardennes style")

ardoise, specials are often written on the *ardoise*, a chalk board.
This can also mean (for regular customers) that they put it
on your running bill

arête, fish bone

argenteuil, asparagus soup

arlequin, two flavors

armagnac, brandy (similar to *cognac*). The main difference is
cognac is distilled twice (& thus smoother)
while *armagnac* is distilled only once

armoricaine, in a tomato sauce

arôme, aroma

aromates, herbs & spices

aromatisé, flavored

artichaut, artichoke

artichauts à la barigoule, artichokes w/mushrooms & pork

artichaut violet, small artichoke

asperge, asparagus

asperge à la flamande, white asparagus w/egg sauce.
A Belgian specialty

asperge d'Argenteuil, large white artichoke

aspic, gelatin

aspic de volaille, chicken in aspic

assaisonnement, dressing/seasoning

assiette, plate

assiette anglaise, cold cuts

assiette de charcuterie, assorted meat products (cold cuts)

assiette de crudités, a plate of raw vegetables

assiette du pêcheur, assorted fish plate

assorti, assorted

asturienne, w/livers

au, in

aubergine, eggplant

aulx, garlic (the plural of *ail*)

Aubergine.

aumônière, *crêpe* filled & wrapped into the shape of a little purse. The word means "beggar's purse"

aurore, a tomato sauce

auvergnat, usually means served w/sausage & cabbage (means "Auvergne style")

aux, with

avec, with

avec des glaçons, on the rocks

avocat, avocado

avoine, oats

aziminu, Corsican *bouillabaisse*

Avec des glaçons.

baba au rhum, spongecake soaked in rum

bäckaoffa, meat & potato stew from Alsace

bacon, Canadian bacon

baeckeoffe, baked meat & potato stew from Alsace

bagna cauda, hot anchovy dip from Provence

baguette, long & thin loaf of bread

baies, berries

baigné, bathed

ballottine (de volaille), boned meat (poultry) stuffed, rolled, cooked & served in gelatin

Ballotine. Not sure about this concept.

banane, banana

bananes flambées, bananas flamed in brandy

bananes vertes, green bananas used in dishes in the French West Indies

Bandol, popular wine from Provence. The red is full-bodied & spicy & the white is fruity, often with a hint of aniseed

banon, cheese from Provence dipped in *eau-de-vie* & wrapped in chestnut leaves

bar, bass

barbarie, Barbary (a type of duck)

barbouiado, vegetable *ragoût*

barbue, brill (fish)

barde, the lard or bacon put over roasts

barigoule, artichoke hearts, sausage, bacon, garlic & mushroom dish

*Barigoule.
like the sound
of it*

baron, the hindquarter & leg of a lamb

barquette, small boat-shaped pastry. *Une barquette* means "a carton of"

Barry, à la du, served w/a cauliflower & cheese sauce

basilic, basil

basquaise, served w/tomatoes, or red peppers ("Basque style")

bâtard, a small *baguette*

batonnets, crisp sticks. *Batonnets de courgette* are crisp zucchini sticks

baudroie, monkfish
This can also refer to a fish soup w/garlic & vegetables

bavaroise, custard dessert

bavette, flank steak

béarnaise, *hollandaise* sauce w/vinegar, tarragon, shallots & wine

Sauce Bearnaise

béatilles, mixed organ meats

beaufort, a hard cheese

Beaujolais, one of France's wine regions (on the south tip of Burgundy) noted for fruity red wines. *Beaujolais Nouveau* is light & fruity & denotes the first wine to be released

beaumont, a mild cheese

bécasse, woodcock

bécassine, snipe

béchamel, white sauce (usually butter, milk [&/or cream] & flour)

beckenoff, pork & mutton baked w/potatoes

beignet, fritter filled w/fruit, meat &/or vegetables (a filled doughnut)

belle étoile, a mild cheese

belon, a type of oyster

*Belle étoile ~
beautiful
star.*

bénédictine, dark green, brandy-based liqueur

bergamotte, a variety of lemon or pear

bercy, fish stock *velouté* w/white wine,
 shallots & parsley

berlingots, mint-flavored caramels

betterave, beet

beuchelle, creamed kidneys &
 sweetbreads

Bettrave.

beurgoule, caramel-rice pudding

beurre, butter

beurre blanc, white butter sauce of
 white wine, vinegar & shallots

beurre blanc nantais, white butter & shallot sauce for fish

beurre d'ail, garlic butter

beurre d'anchois, anchovy butter

beurre de montpellier, green butter (made green from herbs)

beurre d'estragon, tarragon butter

beurre fondu, melted butter

beurre maître d'hôtel, butter w/chopped parsley & lemon juice

beurre manié, butter & flour thickening for sauces

beurre nantais, white butter

beurre noir, browned butter sauce
 (until it's almost black)

beurre noisette, lightly browned butter

bicard de soude, baking soda

biche, female deer

bien cuit, well done

bière, beer

bière à la pression, draft beer

bière blonde, lager beer

Bière.

bière brune, dark beer

bière légère, light beer

bifteck, beef steak

biftek de cheval, horse-meat steak

bigarade, brown sauce usually w/vinegar, sugar & oranges

bigarreau, a type of cherry

bigorneaux, small sea mollusks

bigourneau, the shellfish periwinkle

billes de melons, melon balls

billy bi, cream of mushroom soup

biscotte, zwieback (sweetened bread enriched w/eggs, baked &
 sliced & toasted until dry & crisp)

biscuit, biscuit/cookie
biscuit à la cuillère, ladyfingers
biscuit de Savoie, spongecake
biscuits aux brisures de chocolat,
    chocolate-chip cookies
bisque, chowder
bisque d'écrevisses, freshwater
    crayfish chowder
bisque de homard, lobster bisque
bisque de langoustines, saltwater
    crayfish chowder
blaff, spicy stewed fresh fish
    dish served in the
    French West Indies
blanc, white
blanc-cassis, white wine &
    black currant liqueur
blanc de blancs, white wine made from white grapes
blanc de poireau, the white part of a leek
blanc de volaille, boned breast of poultry
blanchaille, whitebait, a fish
blanchi, blanched
blanquette, stew
blanquette de veau, veal
    stew in a white sauce
blé, wheat
blé de turquie, corn
blé dur, duram wheat
blette, Swiss chard
bleu, blue cheese/meat prepared nearly raw/fish boiled very
    fresh. Some popular blue cheeses
    are bleu d'Auvergne, bleu de Bresse,
    bleu des Causses & bleu du Haut-Jura
blini, small pancakes (usually w/sour
    cream, caviar & salmon)
blonde, light (as in light-colored
    [lager] beer)
boeuf, beef
boeuf à la ficelle, beef cooked in stock
boeuf à la gardiane, beef & wine stew w/black olives
boeuf à la gordienne, braised beef dish from Provence

Bisque de... ecrevisses, homard, Langoustines... Love 'em all.

Blanc Cassis is a popular aperatif in France.

In Canada Blonde means girl friend no matter what color her hair is

boeuf à la mode, beef marinated in red wine

boeuf bourguignon, beef stewed in red wine (burgundy)
w/onions, bacon & mushrooms

boeuf braisé à la beauceronne, beef casserole found
around Orléans

boeuf en daube, larded chunks of beef marinated & cooked in
wine/beef casserole

boeuf miroton, beef stew or boiled beef w/onion sauce

boeuf mode, beef stew w/carrots. This can also refer to cold
beef in jelly

boeuf salé, corned beef

bohémienne, eggplant & tomato casserole. A specialty in Nice

boisson, beverage

boissons compris, drinks included

boissons non compris, drinks not included

boîte, can, box or jar. *Une boîte de conserve...* means a can of...

boles de picolat, meatballs & mushrooms cooked in a sauce

bolet, boletus mushroom

bombe/bombe glacée, layered ice cream

bon, bonne, good

bonbons, candy

bonne femme, homestyle cooking.
This can also refer to a *sauce veloutée* w/*crème
fraîche* & lemon juice

*Bonne femme
means Good
Woman.*

bonnefoy, *sauce velouté* w/shallots & white wine

Bordeaux, one of France's wine regions (the largest wine-
producing area in the world). Red *Bordeaux* is made from a
blend of cabernet sauvignon, merlot, cabernet franc,
malbec & petite verdot grapes. White *Bordeaux* is made
from semillon & sauvignon blanc grapes.

bordelaise, red wine sauce w/mushrooms, beef marrow &
shallots

botte, bunch (as in a bunch of herbs). *Botte de radis* means
bunch of radishes

bouchée, bite size. *Cidre bouché* refers to alcoholic, dry cider

bouchée à la reine, puff pastry filled w/meat, seafood, sweet
breads &/or mushrooms

boucherie, butcher shop. *Boucheries chevalines* are still found
in France & are horse-meat butcher shops

bouchon, cork

boudin, blood sausage (black pudding)

boudin blanc, white sausage
(sausage of white meats)
boudin liège, Belgian sausage
boudin noir (boudin antillais), spicy
blood sausage (a specialty
in the French West Indies)
bougon, a goat's milk cheese
bouillabaisse, shellfish & fish stewed
in white wine, olive oil, saffron,
tomatoes & garlic. There are many versions of this dish
bouilli, boiled/boiled beef
bouillon, broth/stock
boulanger, baker. *Boulangère* is a woman baker
boulangerie, bakery
boule de fromage frit, fried cheese ball
boulette, meatball or fishball
boulette de semoule, semolina & potato *gnocchi*
boulghour, bulgur wheat
boullinade, thick soup found in the South of France
bouquet, large (red) shrimp (usually served cold)
bouquet garni, a small bundle of herbs
&/or spices tied together in
cheesecloth & used to provide
flavor to dishes while they cook
bouquet rose, prawns
bourbon, bourbon
bourboulhade, salt cod & garlic soup.
Sometimes referred to as
a poor man's *bouillabaisse*
bourdaines, apples baked in pastry
bourdaloue, butter cake w/fruit
Bourgogne, Burgundy. Burgundy is one of France's wine
regions (famous for red wines made from pinot noir grapes)
Bourgueil, light, fruity wine from the Loire Valley
bourguignon/bourguignonne, mushrooms & onions in a red
wine sauce (see *boeuf bourguignon*)
bouribut, red wine duck stew
bourride, a fish stew found in the South of France (thickened
w/egg yolks & *aïoli*)
boursin, a mild, soft cheese
boutargue, smoked fish roe

Boudin is also an unflattering term for a woman.

Bouquet garni can be found in boxes packaged like tea bags and are great.

bouteille, bottle

braisé, braised

braiser, to braise

branches de céleri, celery stalks

brandade, cod & potato dish

brandade de morue, salt cod w/garlic, cream & olive oil

brandy, brandy

brebis, sheep's-milk cheese

brème, bream

Bretagne, Brittany, an Atlantic coastal province

bretonne, usually a dish served w/white wine sauce or white beans ("Brittany style"). This can also refer to a type of oyster

brézzolles, slices of veal

bricks, round, paper-thin sheets of pastry (usually filled w/egg & Middle Eastern spices). A specialty of Tunisia

brie, white, mellow, soft cheese. If you don't know what *brie* is, you shouldn't be in France

brins, branches or sprigs

brioche, small sweet cake or roll

broccio, a cheese (similar to *ricotta*) found in Corsica

broche, (on a) spit

brochet, pike

brochette de coeurs, heart kabob. A specialty in Toulouse

brochette, en, cooked on a skewer

brocoli, broccoli

broufado, braised beef w/anchovies

brouillade d'aubergines, stuffed eggplant w/tomatoes

brouillé, scrambled

Brouilly, red wine from Beaujolais

brousse de brebis, soft & mild sheep's- or goat's-milk cheese

brousse du Rove, cheese (similar to *ricotta*) made w/sheep's milk. The sheep graze on thyme, which gives the cheese its unusual flavor

brugnon, nectarine

brûlé, burned/caramelized

brune, dark (as in dark beer)

brunoise, diced vegetables

brut, very dry

Handwritten margin notes: Bouteille ~ Bootay; Brins de romarin; Brugnon.

bûche de Noël, rolled Christmas cake
buffet froid, a variety of cold dishes
bugnes, fried doughnuts
buisson, vegetable dish
bulot, large sea snail
Burgundy, a wine (red, white or rosé) produced in the
    Burgundy region
Byrrh, sweet wine (fortified w/brandy) mixed w/quinine
cabécou, a strong, round goat cheese
Cabernet Sauvignon, dry red wine
cabillaud, cod
cabri, kid goat
cacahuète, peanut
cacao, cocoa
cachat, fresh cheese from Provence
Caen, à la mode de, cooked w/*calvados*
café, coffee (really, espresso)
café américain, American-style coffee
café au lait, coffee w/milk
café brûlot, flaming coffee
    (strong coffee w/liquor
    which is set on fire)
café complet, continental breakfast
    (coffee, bread, butter & jam)
café crème, coffee w/cream
café déca, decaffeinated coffee
café décaféiné, decaffeinated coffee
café de Paris, the name for a butter
    sauce flavored w/cognac & herbs
café espresso, espresso
café express, espresso
café filtre, drip-brewed coffee/
    American-style coffee
café frappé, iced coffee
café glacé, coffee-flavored ice
    cream/iced coffee
café liégeois, cold coffee
    served w/ice cream
café nature, black coffee
café noir, black coffee
café sans caféine, decaffeinated coffee

Bûche de Noël.

Cafe Americain.
←

*If you want
to order
American
coffee without
seeming so...
American, you
can order
Café élongée.
(AY-Lon-jay)
It's just French
coffee "elongated"
with water.*

café soluble, instant coffee

café viennois, coffee w/whipped cream

cagouille, small land snail

caille, quail

caillete, pâté of pork, herbs & garlic

calalou, "pepperpot" stew w/many
ingredients found in the French West Indies

calamar, squid

calissons, marzipan candies
shaped like boats from Aix

calmar, squid

Calmar.

calvados, apple brandy

camembert, soft cheese w/strong flavor

camomille, camomile tea

campagne, à la, this term means "country style" & has many
different meanings

canapé, appetizer w/bread base & topped w/various ingredients

canard, duck

canard à la presse, roast duck dish w/red wine & Cognac

canard à l'orange, roast duck braised w/orange sauce

canard de Barbarie, a duck breed in Southwest France

canard de Challans, a type of small duck

canard de Nantes, a type of small duck   *Canard.*

canard de Rouen, a type of wild duck

canard laqué, Peking duck

canard Montmorency, duck w/cherries

canard rôti, roast duck

canard sauvage, wild duck

cancoillotte, strong, hard cheese (melted before serving) from
the Franche-Comté region in Eastern France

candi, candied

caneton, duckling

canette, young female duck

canistrelli, dry cookies from Corsica

cannelle, cinnamon

cantal, a cheese very much like cheddar

caouanne, turtle

capoun fassum, cabbage stuffed w/rice & sausage

câpre, caper

caqhuse, pork & onion casserole

carafe, carafe

caramélisé, caramelized

caramel, burned sugar. This also refers to a chewy vanilla or chocolate caramel

carapaces, shells

carbonnade, braised beef stew (a Belgian specialty) also charcoal-grilled meat

carbonnade à la boeuf, Belgian specialty of beef marinated in beer & cooked in onions & herbs

carbonnade bruxelloise, Belgian dish of pork w/a tomato & tarragon sauce

carbonnade flamande, beef, herbs & onions braised in beer

carbonnade nîmoise, lamb & potato dish

cardinal, fish stock *velouté*, lobster, butter & cream

cardomome, cardamom

cardon, cardoon (a member of the thistle family)

cargolade, grilled snail dish from Languedoc-Roussillon

cari, curry

carotte, carrot

carottes glacées, carrots glazed in butter

carottes râpées, grated carrots

carottes Vichy, steamed carrots (in butter & parsley)

carpe, carp

carré, rack/loin/fillet

carré d'agneau, rack or loin of lamb

carré de l'Est, pungent cheese (square shaped)

carré de porc, rack or loin of pork

carré de veau, rack or loin of veal

carrelet, flounder/plaice

carte, la, menu

carte des vins, wine list

carvi, caraway seeds

casse-croûte, snack ("breaking the crust")

casse-pierre, seaweed

cassis, black currant/black currant liqueur

cassolette, dish served in a small casserole

cassoulet (toulousain), meat & bean (& often sausage) casserole. This dish originated in Southwest France

castagna, chestnut in Corsican

[handwritten margin note:] Carapaces refers to shrimp or Lobster Shells.

[handwritten margin note:] The French are not so much for snacking, Casse-croute refers to a small-meal type snack.

castanhet, chestnut cake

cavaillon, a fragrant melon from the town of the same name in
Provence. It looks like a small cantaloupe

cave, wine shop/wine cellar

caviar, fish eggs

caviar d'aubergine, eggplant purée

cédrat, citron

céleri, celery

Celeri.

céleri-rave, celery root

céleri rémoulade, celery root in a creamy mayonnaise
dressing

cendre chemisée, smoldering

cèpe, boletus mushroom

céréale, cereal

cerf, venison (deer)

cerfeuil, chervil

cerise, cherry

cerise noire, black cherry

Cerf.

cerises jubilé, cherries flamed w/*kirsch* & served w/ice cream

cerneau, the "meat" of a walnut

cervelas, seasoned sausage made from brains

cervelle, brains

cervelle de canut, herbed cheese spread

chabichou, cow's- & goat's-milk cheese.
Some think it has a sweet flavor

*Cervelle.
Apparently
Some people
like it.*

Chablis, one of France's wine regions producing white wine
made from the chardonnay grape

chair, "fleshy" part of fish or meat

Challonaise, wine region producing mostly table wine

chambré, room temperature (when serving wine)

Champagne, A region in Northeastern France famous
for its sparkling wines classified by the sugar content.
Brut is the driest, ***extra-sec*** is very dry, ***sec*** is
dry, ***demi-sec*** is slightly sweet & ***doux*** is sweet.
Also a sweet cookie served w/champagne

champenoise, sparkling wine

champêtre, this term means "rustic" & can
mean many things – usually it
signifies a simple dish

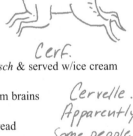

Champignons.

champignon, mushroom

champignon à la grecque, cold mushroom appetizer

champignon de bois, wild mushroom

champignon de Paris, button mushroom

champignon de pin, pine mushroom.
A wild mushroom found in Provence

champignon sauvage, wild mushroom

changement de garniture, this means an extra charge for
substitutions

chansons aux pommes, flaky breakfast
pastry w/apple filling

Chansons aux pommes means Song to apples.

chanterelle, chanterelle mushroom

chantilly, sweet whipped cream.
This can also refer to
hollandaise sauce & whipped cream

chaource, cheese found in the Champagne region

chapelure, breadcrumbs

chapon, capon

chapon de mer, scorpion fish

charbonnade, charcoal-grilled meat

charcuterie, can be a deli or any
place serving prepared meats & salads.
This can also refer to cooked pork meats/cold cuts

charcuterie assortie, assorted cold meats

chariot, dessert &/or cheese cart

Chariot... be on the Lookout!

charlotte, fruit dessert made in a
mold/baked fruit compote/pudding

charolais, denotes a high-quality beef

chartreuse, yellow (or green) herb liqueur. Also a game bird
(usually pheasant or partridge) dish from Alsace

chasse, venison

chasselas, a white grape

chasseur, "hunter's style" usually means
in a sauce w/tomatoes,
wine, herbs & mushrooms

Chasse means hunt.

châtaigne, chestnut

châtaignes chaudes/marrons chauds, roasted chestnuts

chateaubriand, thick slice of tenderloin stuffed w/sauteed
shallots & usually served
w/butter or *béarnaise* sauce

Château-Margaux, red wine from Bordeaux

Châteauneuf-du-Pape, red wine from
the Rhône River valley

Châteauneuf du Pape means the Pope's new castle.

chaud, hot

chaud-froid, cold poultry dish/a
    dish containing gelatin. It's
    cooked & then served cold, thus
    the name which means "hot-cold"

chaudrée, seafood & fish stew
    (contains the white part of squid)

chauffé, heated

chaumes, rich, creamy cheese from Dordogne

chausson, fruit turnover

chausson aux pommes, apple turnover

chemise, en, baked in parchment/wrapped in
    pastry/potato w/the skin left on

cheval, horse

chèvre, goat/goat cheese

chevreau, young goat

chèvre fraîche, goat cheese which is only a few days old

chèvre sèche, dried (aged) goat cheese

chevreuil, deer

chichi, orange-flavored doughnuts/can also mean "fancy"

chicons du Nord, Belgian endive

chicorée, chicory/endive

chicorée frisée, curly lettuce

chicorée witloof, Belgian endive

chiffonnade, shredded leafy vegetables & herbs

chinchard, saurel, a fish

chinois, Chinese

Chinon, red wine from the Loire Valley

chipiron, small squid

chipirons en su tinta, Basque dish of squid
    cooked in its own ink

chipolatas, small sausages

chips, potato chips

chivry, a *béarnaise* sauce w/spinach, parsley or watercress
    added to make it green

chocolat, chocolate

chocolat à la bayonne, chocolate cream dessert

chocolat amer, bitter chocolate

chocolat au lait, milk chocolate

chocolat chaud, hot chocolate

chocolat mi-amer, bittersweet chocolate

Hot Chocolate is more common in Europe than in the U.S.

69

chocolat noir, bitter chocolate/black chocolate

choix, "choice." On a menu, this means you can choose among a list of dishes

chope, large beer

choron, *béarnaise* sauce w/tomatoes

chou, cabbage

chou à la crème, cream puff

choucroute, sauerkraut. In Alsace, this refers to a dish of cabbage w/pork, potatoes & sauerkraut

Love choucroute garni!

choucroute garnie, sauerkraut w/ham, pork sausage or frankfurters

chouée, buttered cabbage dish

Mon petit chou is a term of endearment.

chou-fleur, cauliflower

chou frisé, kale/savoy cabbage

chou marin, kale

chou rouge, red cabbage

chou vert, green cabbage

choux de Bruxelles, brussels sprouts

ciboule, scallion

ciboulette, chive

cidre, cider. Popular in Brittany

cigales, a type of clam

cigarette, sugar cookie (rolled in the shape of a cigarette)

citron, the term for lemons & limes (citrus fruit) but can also simply refer to a lemon

citronelle, lemon grass

citronnade, lemon drink

citron pressé, fresh lemon juice w/sugar & water (lemonade)

citron vert, lime

citrouille, pumpkin

civelles, baby eels

civet, game stew. Popular in Corsica

civet de lapin, rabbit stew

civet de lièvre, hare stew

clafouti, fruit baked in pancake batter *LOVE this*

clafouti du limousin, cherry *clafouti*

claires, oysters (raised in an oyster bed)

clamart, stuffed w/green peas

Claret, dry, red table wine from Bordeaux

clémentine, seedless tangerine

clos, vineyard

clou de girofle, clove

clouté, "studded with"

cocaos, cocoa

cochon, pig

cochon de lait, suckling pig *Cochon.*

cochon de lait en gelée, suckling pig in aspic *I'll pass.*

cochonnailles, assorted pork sausages & pâtés

cocotte, casserole *Cocotte.*

coeur, heart

coeur d'artichaut, artichoke heart

coeur de filet, thickest & best part of a beef filet

coeurs de palmiers, hearts of palm served w/a mustard
vinaigrette

cognac, cognac

coing, quince

Cointreau, orange-flavored liqueur

colbert, à la, dipped in batter & breadcrumbs & fried

colin, hake

colonel, lemon sherbet w/vodka

colvert, wild duck

complet, full/whole

compote, stewed fruit

compote de..., stewed

compris, included

comté, a mild cheese (similar to the Swiss gruyère cheese)

concassé, chopped

concentré, concentrate

concombre, cucumber

concorde, chocolate meringue & chocolate mousse

condiments, seasoning

confiserie, candy & sweets shop

confit, goose, pork, turkey or duck preserved in fat.
Also vegetables/fruit preserved in alcohol, sugar or vinegar

confiture, jam/preserves.
Confiture d'oignons is onion compote

confiture de vieux garçon, fruit served in alcohol

confiture d' orange, marmalade

congre, conger eel

consommation, drinks

consommé, broth (clear soup)

Vieux Garçon means Old boy. Something like old maid.

consommé aux vermicelles, broth w/thin noodles
consommé Célestine, broth w/chicken & noodles
consommé colbert, broth w/vegetables & poached eggs
consommé madrilène, cold broth w/tomatoes
consommé princesse, broth w/chicken & asparagus
consultez aussi l'ardoise, other suggestions
   on the blackboard
consultez notre carte des desserts, consult our dessert menu
contre-filet, sirloin
copeaux, shavings (of vegetables or chocolate)
copieux, filling
coppa, fillet (in Corsica)
coq, rooster
coq au vin, chicken stewed in red wine
   w/bacon, onions, mushrooms & herbs
coq de bruyère, grouse
coque, tiny shellfish (similar to a clam)
coquelet, cockerel
coquillage, shellfish
coquille, shell/scallop
coquille Saint-Jacques, scallops (prepared w/a
   parsley butter or a cream sauce)
coquilles à la nantaise, scallops w/onions.
   A specialty in Brittany
corail, the egg sac of lobster,
   crayfish or scallops
corbeille, basket
corbeille de fruits, basket of assorted fruits
cordon bleu, veal slices stuffed w/ham &
   gruyere, breaded & fried in butter
coriandre, coriander
cornet de frites, paper cone filled
   w/french fries. A popular snack
cornets de murat, cones filled w/cream
cornichon, small pickle (gherkin)
corniottes, cheese pastries made in the shape of hats
corps, refers to the "body" of wine
corsoise, à la, this means that the dish is prepared
   as it would be in Corsica
cosse, pod/husk
côte, rib/chop

Coq au vin grtta have it in Paris

Coquille.

Corbeille.

côte d'agneau, lamb chop

Côte de Beaune, red & white wines from Beaune in Burgundy

côte de boeuf, beef rib steak/T-bone steak

Côte de Nuits, a heavy red Burgundy wine

côte de veau, veal chop

côtelette, cutlet/chop

côtelette d'agneau, lamb chop

côtelette de porc, pork chop

Côtes du Rhône, wine region producing wines such as
Châteauneuf-du-Pape, Côte-Rotie, Hermitage & Tavel

côtes levées, spareribs

cotignac, caramelized apple tart

cotriade, fish stew (from Brittany)

cou, neck

cou d'oie farci, a "sausage" made of the neck skin of a goose
which is stuffed w/meat & spices

couennes de porc, fresh pork rinds

coulibiac, salmon *pâté*

coulis, vegetable, shellfish or fruit purée

coulis de tomates, thick tomato sauce

coulommiers, a mild cheese (similar to *brie*)

coupe, goblet/scoop/a dish used for serving dessert

coupe Danemark, a scoop of vanilla ice
cream covered w/hot chocolate sauce

coupe de champagne, a flute of champagne

Coupe de Champagne.

coupe des îles, a scoop of vanilla ice cream
w/fruit & whipped cream

coupe glacée, ice cream dessert (often a sundae)

courge, squash

courgette, zucchini

courgettes au broccio, *broccio* cheese-stuffed
zucchini dish from Corsica

couronne, circle-shaped or ring-shaped bread

Couronne means crown or wreath.

court bouillon, seafood broth

couscous, Moroccan specialty of steamed grain, broth, meats,
vegetables & other ingredients

couscous royal, *couscous* w/meat

cousinat, bean, bell pepper, artichoke, tomato, green onion &
carrot dish

couteau, knife

Couteau — coo·toe.

couvert, cover charge/place setting

couvert, vin et service compris, the price includes wine, tip & cover charge

crabe, crab

crabe verte, shore crab

crapaudine, grilled game or poultry dish

craquelins, cookies

Crécy, à la, served w/carrots

crème, cream/creamy soup/creamy dessert. Can also refer to sweet liqueur as in *crème de menthe*. *À la crème* means served w/a cream sauce

crème à la vanille, vanilla custard

crème allégée, light cream

crème anglaise, custard

crème brûlée, custard dessert topped w/caramelized sugar

crème caramel, vanilla custard w/caramel sauce

crème catalane, caramel-covered trifle w/cinnamon & anise

crème champignons, cream of mushroom soup

crème chantilly, vanilla-flavored & sweetened whipped cream

crème d'asperges, cream of asparagus soup

crème de cacao, cocoa-flavored liqueur

crème de cassis, black currant liqueur

crème de marrons, chestnut purée

crème de menthe, mint-flavored liqueur

crème de poireaux, cream of leek soup

crème de poulet, cream of chicken soup

crème de volaille, cream of chicken soup

crème épaisse, heavy cream

crème fouettée, whipped cream

crème fraîche, thick, heavy cream

crème frit, fried cream custard dessert from Burgundy

crème glacée, ice cream

crème pâtissière, custard filling in cakes & pastry

crème plombières, custard filled w/fresh fruit

crème renversée, custard dessert in a mold

crèmerie, store selling dairy products

cremets, cream made in molds w/fruit

crêpe, crepe (thin pancake). Popular in Brittany

crêpe froment, buckwheat crepe w/sweet filling

crêpe Suzette, crepe w/orange sauce, flamed w/orange liqueur

crépine, caul fat (fat covering the intestines) used to wrap *pâtés* & *terrines*

We like anything with crème attached.

crépinette, small sausage patty wrapped in caul fat

cresson, watercress

cressonade, watercress sauce

cressonière, watercress soup

crête de coq, cock's comb *YES, they eat this.*
(the fleshy crest on the head of fowl)

creuse, a type of oyster

crevette, shrimp

crevette grise, gray, small shrimp

crevette rose, red shrimp w/firm flesh

cristallisés, crystallized

crist-marine, algae

croissant, crescent-shaped flaky breakfast
roll made of flour, eggs & butter

croquant, crispy

croquants, crispy honey or almond cookies

croque madame, toasted ham &
cheese sandwich topped w/an egg

croquembouche, cream-puff tree *Croquembouche. Typically served at weddings.*

croque monsieur, toasted ham
& cheese sandwich

croquette, ground meat, fish or vegetables
coated in bread crumbs & deep fried

crosse, shank

crottin/croutin de chavignol, a firm
goat cheese

croustade, pie filled w/meat, seafood &/or vegetables

croustillant, crisp/spicy

croûte, crust *— yes, please.*

croûte au fromage, melted cheese served on a slice of toast

croûte de sel, en, in a salt crust

croûte, en, in a pastry crust

croûte forestière, mushrooms on toast

croûtes, croutons

croûton, small toasted piece of bread, usually served in a salad

cru, raw. On a wine list, this means vintage

cru classé, high-quality wine

crudités, raw vegetables *cuiller ~*

crustacé, shellfish (crustaceans) *Qui-air*

cuiller, spoon

cuillère, à la, a dish eaten w/a spoon

cuisine, there are four categories of French cuisine:

Cuisine campagnarde (also known as
cuisine des provinces):
Traditional regional dishes prepared
with fresh ingredients.

Cuisine bourgeoise: French home cooking.

Haute cuisine: An elaborate meal with many
courses featuring
rich and fresh ingredients.

Nouvelle cuisine: Light sauces and small portions that
emphasize the colors and textures of the ingredients.

cuisse, leg & thigh (denotes dark meat)

cuisse de poulet, chicken drumstick w/thigh

cuisses de grenouilles, frogs' legs

cuissot, haunch of game or veal

cuit, cooked

cuit à la vapeur, steamed

cuit au four, baked

cul, haunch

cul de veau, veal pot roast

culotte, rump

cumin, cumin

curaçao, orange-flavored liqueur

curcuma, the spice turmeric (used in curry powder)

cure-dent, (served w/a) toothpick

currie/curry, curry

cuvée, blend of wines or champagne/house wine

Cynar, aperitif w/an artichoke base

darne, thick fillet of fish (often salmon)

dartois, pastry w/jam

datte, date

daube, stew

daube à la niçoise, beef or lamb stew w/red wine,
tomatoes & onions

daube de boeuf, beef stew

daube provençal, gravy w/capers, garlic & anchovies

dauphinois, a mild cheese

daurade, white fish (usually served grilled) found in the South
of France (sea bream)

déca, decaf

décaféiné, decaffeinated

Cuisse ~
Kweece
is dark
meat

déca ~ day-cah

76

décortiqué, shelled/peeled

déglacée, warmed up

dégustation, sampling/tasting

déjeuner, lunch

délice, a delight/a treat

délimité de qualité supérieure, on a wine bottle, this means a
superior-quality wine

demi, half/small beer

demi-bouteille, half bottle

demi-deuil, usually means served w/truffles

demidoff, w/vegetables

demi-glace, beef-stock sauce

demi-sel, soft, salty cream cheese/salted butter

demi-sec, medium dry

demoiselle de Cherbourg, small lobster

denté, dentex (fish)

désossé, boned

dessert, dessert

diable, hot, spicy sauce (often, a strong mustard sauce)/
devilled.) This is also the term for an unglazed, porous pot
used to cook vegetables

diabolo, a drink usually mixed w/lemonade

diane, a brown sauce w/vinegar & peppercorns

dieppoise, shrimp & mussels served in a white wine sauce

digestif, after-dinner drink

dijonnaise, served w/mustard

dinde, turkey

dindon, turkey

dindonneau, young turkey

dîner, dinner

diplomate, custard dessert w/spongecake,
crystallized fruit & topped w/liqueur

discrétion, when you see this on a
menu, it means that you can
drink as much wine as you want
(for a fixed price)

divine, *hollandaise* sauce w/sherry

dodine de canard, stuffed-duck dish

domaine, on a wine label this notes
a high-quality wine

dorade, Mediterranean sea bass

[handwritten margin notes:] demi-bouteille ~ deh-mee· boo-tay

[handwritten margin notes:] dinde ~ dand / dindon ~ dan-dong / dindonea ~ dandon-oh

doré(e), golden

dos, back

dos et ventre, both sides (means "back & front")

douce, sweet

doucette, salad green (a cousin of *mâche*)

douceurs, desserts

doux, mild, sweet

douzaine, dozen

dragées, candied almonds

Dubonnet, wine & brandy-based aperitif w/herbs

duchesse, potatoes mixed w/egg & forced through a pastry tube

dugléré, a white sauce w/tomatoes, shallots & white wine

duxelles, finely chopped sautéed mushrooms

eau, water

eau au syphon, w/seltzer water

eau avec gaz, carbonated water

eau de source, spring water

eau-de-vie, brandy made from
distilled fruit juice. Sold in
elaborate tall & thin bottles in Alsace. The term means
"water of life." This can also refer to any spirit

*Don't worry
you can drink
the water
in France.*

eau du robinet, tap water

eau glacée, iced water

eau minérale, mineral water

eau minérale gazeuse, carbonated mineral water

eau nature, tap water

eau plate, still (not sparkling) water

eau sans gaz, water w/out carbonation

écailler, oyster opener/fish scaler

échalote, shallot

échine, spareribs

éclair, pastry filled w/vanilla custard & topped
w/chocolate icing

écrevisse, crayfish

écrevisse à la nage, crayfish
in a white wine sauce

édam français, nutty-flavored,
orange-colored cheese
originally from the Netherlands

Ecrevisse.

édulcorant, artificial sweetener

effilée, thinly sliced

effiloché, thinly sliced

églefin, haddock

emballé, wrapped

embeurré, buttered/buttery

embeurrée de chou, buttered cabbage

émincé, slices of cooked meat in gravy/anything thinly sliced

émincé de veau, sauteed veal slices w/creme sauce

emmental, Swiss cheese

emporter, à, take-out foods

émulsionné, liquified

*Sounds good.
Never had it.*

enchaud de porc à la périgourdine, pork loin stuffed ⟵
    w/truffles. A specialty in Southwest France

encornet, small squid

endive, endive/chicory

enrubanne, layered dish
    (looks like ribbons)

entier, whole

entrecôte, rib-eye steak

entrecôte Bercy, steak w/wine sauce

Endive.

entrecôte maître d'hôtel, rib-eye steak served w/herb butter

entrecôte marchand de vin, rib-eye steak served in
    red wine sauce

Entre-Deux-Mers, a region of Bordeaux
    that produces white wine

entrée, first course/appetizer

entremets, dessert

épaule, shoulder

épeautre, a variety of wheat

éperlan, smelt

épice, spice

épicé, peppered/spicy

épicerie, small grocery store

épi de maïs, miniature corn
    on the cob (often pickled)

épinard, spinach

épinards en branches, leaf spinach

*Be sure to visit
a grocery
store ~ small
or large,
they're worth
the trip.*

époisse, a cow's-milk cheese from Burgundy

érable, maple

escabèche, raw fish marinated in lime juice & herbs. In
    Provence, this can refer to a cold marinated sardine dish

escalope, scallop/cutlet

escalope de veau, veal scallop
escalope panée, breaded veal scallop
escalope viennoise, breaded veal
    cutlet (weiner schnitzel)
escargot, snail
escargot de mer, sea snail
escargot petit-gris, small snail

Escargot.

escarole, a type of *endive*
espadon, swordfish
essence, essence
estocaficada, cod stew
estofat de boeuf, beef stew
estouffade, beef stew. Can also refer to a steamed dish
estouffados, almond butter cookies found in Provence
estragon, tarragon
esturgeon, sturgeon
et, and

Estragon.

étrille, small crab
étouffée, stewed
étuvé/étuvée, steamed
éventail, en, cut into a fan shape
express, espresso
extra-sec, very dry (champagne)
façon, in the manner of
faisan, pheasant

faisan

faisan normand, pheasant w/apples & *calvados*
faisselle, fresh cow's-milk cheese
fait à la maison, homemade
falette, stuffed breast of veal
far, prune tart
farandole, dessert &/or cheese cart
farce, spiced ground meat (usually pork) used for stuffing
farci, stuffed, as in ***chou farci*** (stuffed cabbage)
      & ***tomates farcies*** (stuffed tomatoes).
    In Nice, this is a dish of   ⟵   love these
    stuffed vegetables
farigoule, the name in Provence for wild thyme
farine, flour
farine de blé, wheat flour
farine de maïs, corn flour
faux-filet, flank steak/sirloin steak

fécule, starch. ***Fécule de pommes de terre*** is potato flour used
    to thicken sauces & soups

fécule de maïs, cornstarch

fendant, "melting." Refers to extremely tender meat
    or chocolate

fenouil, fennel

féra, dace (lake salmon)

ferme, farm/farm fresh

fermier, poultry raised on a farm

feu de bois, cooked on a wood fire

feuille, leaf

feuille de chêne, oak-leaf lettuce

feuille de laurel, bay leaf

feuille de vigne, vine leaf

feuilles farcies, grape leaves stuffed w/rice & herbs

feuilletage, puff pastry

feuilletée, puff pastry

fève, broad bean

fiadone, cheesecake found in Corsica

ficelle, small baguette. ***Ficellé*** means tied w/a string

figatelli, Corsican liver sausage

figue, fig

figue de barbarie, prickly pear

filet, fillet

filet à la mistral, filet of sole w/tomatoes & mushrooms

filet de boeuf, beef fillet

filet de boeuf à la Poitou, beef fillet w/chicken liver *pâté*

filet de boeuf Bordelaise, beef fillet in a red wine sauce

filet de sole, fillet of sole

filet de sole meunière, fillet of sole fried in butter

filet doria, fillet of sole w/cucumbers

filet mignon, small round beef tenderloin fillet

filet Saint-Germain, fillet of sole w/potatoes

financière, cream & Madeira wine sauce. This can also refer to
    a dish w/veal or chicken dumplings

fine, a fine brandy

fines de claire, oysters

fines herbes, mixture of herbs (such as parsley, chives, tarragon
    & thyme)

flageolets, small kidney-shaped beans

flagnarde/flaugnarde, fruit-filled cake

Feu de bois on a sign outside a restaurant indicates that they cook with wood.

ficelle means string.

figues.

flamande, à la, "Flemish style" w/potatoes, stuffed cabbage leaves, vegetables, sausage & bacon

flambé(e), flaming

flamiche, savory tart (similar to a quiche)

flan, tart or crustless pie. Can also refer to the caramel custard dessert of the same name found in Spain

flanchet, flank

flet, flounder

flétan, halibut

fleur, flower. *Fleurs* are crystallized flowers used on desserts

fleurette, small flower

Fleurie, a red wine from Beaujolais

fleurons, crescent-shaped puff pastries

fleurs de courgettes farcies, zucchini flowers stuffed w/cheese

flocon, flake

flocons d'avoine, oat flakes

florentine, w/spinach

foie, liver

foie de veau, calf's liver

foie de veau grand-mère, sautéed calf's liver w/bacon, onion & potato garnish

foie de volaille, chicken liver

foie gras, fattened goose liver

foie gras de canard, fattened duck liver

foie gras d'oie, fattened goose liver

foie gras en brioche, fattened goose liver that is marinated & cooked & baked a second time in a pastry shell

foies blonds de volaille, chicken livers

foin, cooked in hay ⟵ *I'd rather not.*

fond, bottom

fondant, cake icing

fondant au chocolat, similar to a brownie (but better!)

fond d'artichaut, artichoke heart

fondu/fondue (au fromage), melted cheese in a pot. Dip your bread or meat in!

fondu aux raisins, the crust of this smooth & creamy cheese is made of grape pulp. Also known as ***tomme au marc***

fondue bourguignonne, small pieces of meat dipped into oil & eaten w/sauces

fondue chinoise, thin slices of beef dipped in bouillon & eaten w/sauces

fondue savoyarde, pot of melted cheese for dipping

forestière, ("forester's style") usually means w/sautéed
mushrooms

forêt noire, Black Forest cake

forme d'Ambert, a blue cheese

formule, une, a set-price menu

fort, strong (as in strong or sharp cheese)

fougasse, decorated bread loaf w/olive oil flavoring &
sometimes w/bacon, onion or tomato stuffing

fougassette, a slice of *brioche* bread flavored
w/orange & saffron

four, au, baked

fourchette, fork

fournée, baked

fournitures, fresh herbs & salad greens

fourré, filled/stuffed

fraîche, fresh

frais, fresh

fraise, strawberry

[handwritten: Fraîche – fraysh / Frais – fray / Fraise – freZ]

fraise des bois, wild strawberry

framboise, raspberry/raspberry liqueur

frangipane, almond custard filling

frappé, drink blended w/ice

frémis, oysters (served almost raw)

friand, meat-filled pastry

friandises, *petits fours*

fricadelles, fried meat patties

fricadelles à la bière, meatballs in beer. A specialty in Belgium

fricandeau, braised veal dish

fricassée, a stew of meat, poultry or fish finished w/cream

fricassée liégeoise, fried eggs, bacon & sausage. A specialty in
Belgium

frigolet, name in Provence for wild thyme

frisée, curly endive

frit, fried

fritelli, chestnut-flour doughnuts from Corsica

frites, french fries (often eaten w/mayonnaise) *[handwritten: ← yes!]*

fritons, minced spread made of organ meats *[handwritten: ← No.!]*

fritot, batter fried or fritter

friture, frying

friture de mer/friture de poisson, fried small fish

froid, cold

Froid ~ Fwa

fromage, cheese. It is said that
there are over 400 different French cheeses

fromage à pâte dure, hard cheese

fromage à pâte molle, soft cheese

fromage au marc, a sharp, tangy cheese

fromage blanc, cream cheese (but runny)

fromage de brebis, sheep's-milk cheese

fromage de chèvre, goat's-milk cheese

*I don't
think so.*

fromage de tête, headcheese (sausage made from the meat of a
calf's or pig's head cooked in a gelatinous meat
broth & then served cold)

fromage fermier, cheese made where the milk is produced

fromage fort, extremely soft cheese from Provence mixed
w/herbs, salt, pepper & *marc*

fromage maigre, low-fat cheese

fromagerie, cheese shop

fruit, fruit

Fruit ~ fru-ee

fruit confit, candied fruit

fruit de la passion, passion fruit

fruits de mer, seafood

fumé, smoked

fumet, fish stock

galantine, cold gelatinized meat dish

galette, buckwheat pancake. *Galettes de blé de sarrasin* are
crêpes made w/dark flour and filled w/cheese, ham,
an egg, mushrooms or any number of things.
Galettes de blé de froment are dessert crêpes made with
light flour. *Galette* can also refer to a flaky pastry "cake"
w/an almond paste filling. This is the traditional cake served
on Three Kings' Day. A bean (now a little porcelain statue is
used) is put in the cake & the person who gets the piece
containing the bean is king or queen for the day & wears a
a gold crown

galette bretonne, butter & rum cake

galette de pommes, apple tart

galette de sarrasin, buckwheat pancake w/savoury filling
popular in Brittany

galopin, bread pancake

Gamay de Touraine, red wine made w/the Gamay grape

gambas, large prawns

gambas à la planxa, grilled shrimp served on a plank of wood

ganses, fried cakes topped w/sugar

garbure, cabbage soup. In Southern France, this is usually cabbage soup w/ham

garni(e), w/vegetables/garnished

garniture, vegetables/garnished

gâteau, cake

gâteau au chocolat, chocolate cake

gâteau au fromage, cheese tart

gâteau de Savoie, spongecake

gâteau de riz, rice pudding

gateau ~ gat-oh

gaufre, waffle. A specialty in Belgium

gaufrette, sweet wafer

gayettes, small sausage patties

gazeuse, carbonated.
Non-gazeuse means not carbonated

gelé, frozen

gelée, jellied/in aspic

gélinotte, prairie chicken

genièvre, juniper berry

génoise, spongecake

Gelée. Hmmm. not something we eat with gusto.

germiny, sorrel & cream soup/w/sorrel

gésier, gizzard

Gewürztraminer, dry white wine from Alsace

gibelotte de lapin, rabbit stew

gibier, game

gigot, leg

gigot d'agneau, leg of lamb

gigot de mer, oven-roasted monkfish dish

gigot de mouton pré-salé, leg of lamb dish made w/lambs that graze in salt meadows in Northwest France

gigot farci, stuffed leg of lamb

gigue, the haunch of game meat

gimblettes, ring cookies

gin, gin

gingembre, ginger

gin tonique, gin & tonic

girofle, clove

girolle, chanterelle mushroom

glaçage, frosting

glace, ice/ice cream

glacé, iced/glazed

glace à la napolitaine, layers of different-flavored ice cream

glace au fondant, shiny cake icing

glace crémeuse, ice cream

glace de viande, concentrated meat stock (meat glaze)

glace de poisson, concentrated fish stock

glaçons, ice

globe, round (cut of meat)

gnocchi, gnocchi (potato dumplings). Found frequently on menus in Nice & near the Italian border

gnocchi aux blettes, gnocchi w/Swiss chard incorporated into the dough

gougère, cheese-flavored pastry ⟵ *Oui, s'il vous plaît.*

goujon, gudgeon (related to carp)

goujonnettes, small slices of fish

gourmandises, sweets/candies

gousse, clove

gousse d'ail, clove of garlic

goûter, snack/to taste

graine, grain/seed

graine de maïs, corn meal

graine de moutarde, mustard seed

graines de paradis, similar to the spice cardamom & found in the former French African colonies

graisse, fat

graisserons, fried pieces of goose or duck skin *Graisserons. These are like cracklings and used as garnish.*

grand, large

grand crème, a large milky coffee

grand cru, high-quality wine

Grand Marnier, orange liqueur

grand-mère, means "grandmother." A garnish usually of mushrooms, potatoes & bacon

grand veneur, brown sauce w/red currants (usually served w/game)

grand vin, high-quality wine

granité, slushy iced drink

gras, fat/fatty

gras-double, tripe simmered in wine & onions

gratin, au, topped w/grated cheese, breadcrumbs & butter & then baked

gratin dauphinois, potato au gratin dish w/eggs, cheese & cream

gratin de fruits de mer, shellfish in a cream sauce

gratin de queues d'écrevisses, freshwater crayfish served *au gratin*

gratin de capucins, *gratin* of stuffed artichoke hearts

gratin savoyard, baked sliced-potato casserole

gratiné, prepared w/breadcrumbs

gratinée, topped w/cheese/onion soup

grattons, fried pieces of pork, goose or duck skin

gratuit, free

Graves, wine region of Bordeaux

grecque, cold vegetable mixture (*légumes à la grecque*). *À la grecque* refers to dishes stewed in oil (in the Greek style)

grelot, small white onion

grenade, pomegranate

grenadin, small veal scallop

grenoblois, caramel-walnut cake

grenouille, frog

gribiche, mayonnaise w/gherkins & capers. *Sauce gribiche* can refer to a vinaigrette & egg sauce

grillade, grilled meat/mixed grill

grillé, grilled

griotte, a type of cherry (usually in white alcohol)

Grenouille.

grive, thrush (a bird)

grondin, spiked-headed ocean fish (gurnet)

gros bout de poitrine, brisket

groseille, currant

groseille à maquereau, gooseberry/currant

groseille rouge, red currant

gros sel, coarse salt

grumes, heavy coating or skin

Gruyère

gruyère, Swiss cheese

guimauve, marshmallow

haché, hashed

hachis, hash

hachis parmentier, shepherd's pie (ground meat & mashed potatoes topped w/a white sauce & served in a casserole)

hareng, herring

harengs fumés à la Créole, spicy smoked herring dish flamed in rum (found in the French West Indies)

haricot, bean

haricot de mer, tiny clam

haricot de mouton, mutton, bean & potato stew

haricot de soisson, navy bean/kidney bean

haricot rouge, red kidney bean

haricots en salade, bean salad

haricots verts, green beans (french beans)

Henri IV, artichoke hearts & *béarnaise* sauce

herbes, herbs

herbes de Provence, mixture of herbs that includes fennel, lavender, marjoram, bay leaf, sage, rosemary & thyme

hérisson de mer, sea urchin

hochepot, oxtail stew *We like the name.*

hollandaise, sauce of melted butter, egg yolks & lemon juice

homard, lobster

homard à l'américaine, flaming lobster dish w/white wine, herbs, tomatoes & garlic

homard à l'armoricaine, lobster in a tomato sauce

homard cardinal, flaming lobster dish w/mushrooms & truffles

homard froid à la parisienne, cold lobster garnished w/diced vegetables in a mayonnaise sauce

homard Newburg, lobster cooked in a sauce made of butter, cream, wine (or brandy) & egg yolks

homard Thermidor, flaming lobster dish w/white wine, herbs, spices & mustard

hongroise, served w/paprika & cream (means "Hungarian")

hors-d'oeuvre, appetizer

huile, oil

huile d'arachide, peanut oil

huile de carthame, safflower oil

huile de noix, walnut oil

huile de soya, soybean oil

huile de tournesol, sunflower oil

huile d'olive (vierge), olive oil (virgin)

huître, oyster

huître belon, pink oyster

huître portugaise, Portuguese lobster (small & fat)

hure de porc, pig's head

Haricots.

Hors d'oeuvre. means without work.

hure de saumon, salmon pâté
hysope, the bitter herb hysop
île flottante, meringues floating in a cream sauce
impératrice, rice-pudding dessert
importée, imported

île flottante... don't see the appeal of this but it's very popular.

indienne, w/curry (in the style of India)
infusion, herbal tea
jalousies, apricot pastry
jambe, leg
jambon, ham
jambon à l'os, baked ham
jambon blanc, boned, cooked ham
jambon cuit, cooked ham

à l'os means bone-in.

jambon cuit d'Ardennes, smoked ham found in Belgium
jambon de Bayonne, raw, salty ham
jambon de canard, cured, salted or smoked duck or goose breast
jambon de montagne, local cured ham
jambon de Paris, lightly salted ham
jambon de Parme, Parma ham (prosciutto)
jambon de pays, local "country" cured ham
jambon de York, smoked ham (English style)
jambon d'oie, cured, salted or smoked duck or goose breast
jambon cru, cured ham
jambonneau, pork knuckle
jambon persillé, parsleyed ham ←

Never warmed up to this

jardinière, w/diced vegetables
jarret, shank/knuckle
jarret de veau, veal shank (usually a stew)
jerez, sherry (Spanish for sherry)
Jésus de Morteau, smoked pork sausage
jeune, young/green (as in unripe)
joue, cheek
jour, du, of the day
jud mat gardebóneh, smoked pork & bean dish found in Luxembourg
julienne, vegetables cut into fine strips. There is also a fish w/this name
jumeau, pot roast

Jura, one of France's wine-growing regions
jus, juice/gravy
jus de tomate, tomato juice
jus d'orange, orange juice
kaki, persimmon
kalouga, chocolate-pudding cake
ketchup, ketchup
kig-ha-farz, buckwheat pudding
    w/vegetables & meat
kir, apéritif made w/*crème de cassis* & wine
kir royal, apéritif made w/champagne & *crème de cassis*
kirsch, cherry-flavored liqueur
kougelhopf/kouglof/kugelhopf, Alsatian cake w/raisins
    & almonds
kouigh amann, buttered pastry
l', la, le, the (singular). *Les* is the (plural)
lait, milk
laitance, fish roe
lait de beurre, buttermilk
lait écrémé, skim milk
lait entier, whole milk
laitue, lettuce
lambi, conch found in the French West Indies
lamelle, very thin slice
lamproie, lamprey
langouste, crayfish
langouste à la sètoise, lobster (crawfish) w/garlic, tomatoes &
    cognac
langoustine, prawn
langue, tongue
langue de chat, biscuit & ice-cream dessert
Languedoc, one of France's wine-growing regions
languedocienne, usually means eggplant,
    tomato & mushroom garnish
lapereau, young rabbit
lapin, rabbit
lapin à l'artésienne, rabbit stew
lapin à la Lorraine, rabbit in a
    mushroom & cream sauce
lapin aux pruneaux, rabbit w/prunes.
    A popular dish in Northern France

Jus d'orange is usually served with water and sugar.

Lamproie — yikes.

Langue de chat means cat's tongue.

Lapin sworn enemy of all gardeners.

90

lapin chasseur, rabbit in a white wine & herb sauce
lapin de garenne, wild rabbit
lapin en paquets, rabbit pieces in a packet
    of bacon. A specialty in Provence
lard, bacon
lardon, diced bacon
laurier, bay leaf

Laurier.

lavande, lavender. Lavender blossoms are added to dishes in
    Provence such as *sorbet de lavande* (lavender sorbet)
lèche, thin slice (usually of meat or bread)
léger, light
légère, light (as in light beer)
légumes, vegetables
lentilles, lentils
levraut, young rabbit
levure, yeast
libre service, self-service
lieu, small saltwater fish
lièvre, rabbit (hare)
lièvre en cabessal, stuffed hare dish
limande, dab (flounder)
limande sole, lemon sole
limonade, lemonade-flavored soft drink

Limonade is a carbonated soft drink.

liqueur, liqueur
lisette, small mackerel
lit, bed (as in a bed of lettuce)
litre, liter. Wine is often served in a liter carafe, *demi-litre*
    (half-liter) or *un quart* (quarter-liter)
livarot, round, sharp, tangy cheese
Loire, this valley is one of France's wine regions along the
    Loire River
longe, loin. *Longe de veau* is loin of veal
longeole, pork sausage stuffed w/cabbage, leeks & spinach.
    A specialty in French-speaking Switzerland
lonzu, shoulder (in Corsica)
lorraine, usually braised in red wine w/cabbage
lotte, monkfish
loubine, fish similar to sea bass
lou cachat, crushed cheese
lou magret, breast of fattened goose or duck
lou mäis, corn-meal cake found in Provence

Lou means "the" in Provencal.

loup/loup de mer, sea bass. *Loup au fenouille* is sea bass grilled over fennel stalks

lou pevre, goat's-milk cheese w/coarsely ground pepper

lou piech, stuffed veal dish found around Nice

louvine, fish similar to sea bass

Lucullus, dish that contains extremely rich &/or rare ingredients. Named after a Roman general who hosted great feasts

lyonnaise, sautéed w/mushrooms &/or onions/sauce of onions, butter & white wine ("Lyon style")

macaron, macaroon. Not the sticky coconut version found at home, but two almond-meringue cookies, flavored with vanilla, chocolate, coffee, pistachio or other flavors, stuck together with butter cream

macaroni au gratin, macaroni & cheese

macédoine, mixed fruit or mixed vegetables

macédoine de légumes, mixed vegetables

macérer, to pickle or soak

mâche, a type of lettuce

macis, the outer covering of a nutmeg/mace

mache.

Mâcon, wine from Burgundy

mâconnaise, usually refers to a goat's milk cheese

macreuse, pot roast

madeleine, butter cake

madère, w/Madeira wine

magret, breast of fattened goose or duck

maigre, lean

maïs, corn

maison, house

maître d'hôtel, head waiter/sautéed in butter w/lemon juice & parsley

maltaise, orange-flavored *hollandaise* sauce

mandarine, tangerine

mange-tout, snow pea/type of apple

mangue, mango

manière, de, in the style of

maquereau, mackerel

mange-tout means eat all

maraîchère, usually means w/various greens (market style)

marbré, marbled

marc, a strong liqueur made from distilling the residue of grapes (similar to Italian *grappa*). *Marc de Bandol* is a popular *marc* found in Provence

marcassin, young wild boar

marchand de vin, red wine & shallot sauce/wine merchant

marché, market

marée, a term used to denote fresh seafood (literally "the tide")

Marengo, à la, w/eggs

marennes, flat-shelled oysters

margarine, margarine (almost never served in Paris)

Margaux, a red wine from Bordeaux

mariné, marinated

marinière, "sailor's style" usually means w/seafood (most
often mussels) simmered in herbs & white wine

marjolaine, marjoram. This can also refer to a layered
chocolate & nut cake

marmelade, marmalade

marmite, food cooked in a small casserole

marquise, mousse cake

maroilles, strong, hard cheese

marron, chestnut

Marquise... don't miss having this.

marrons au sirop, chestnuts in vanilla-flavored syrup

marrons chauds, roasted chestnuts.
Served on the streets of Paris

marrons entiers au naturel, chestnuts in water
(used in stuffing, sauces or as a vegetable)

marrons glacés, candied chestnuts

marrons Mont Blanc, chestnut purée
& cream on a spongecake soaked in rum

marrons ~ have never seen the appeal of these.

massepain, marzipan

matafan, simple cake (flour, butter, milk & eggs) made in a
skillet

matelote, freshwater fish stew/fish stew (usually eel) w/wine
from the French West Indies. *Matelote de veau* is veal stew
w/red wine

mauresque, a drink of *pastis* w/almond & orange syrup

mauviette, meadow lark

mayonnaise, mayonnaise

médaillon, small, round cut of meat

Médoc, red wine from Bordeaux

mélange, mixture/blend

mélasses, molasses

méli-mélo, assorted seafood

méli-mélo de légumes, mixed vegetables

melon, cantaloupe

melon à l'italienne, melon w/*prosciutto*

melon d'eau, watermelon. The French call it ***pastèque***

melon de Cavaillon, similar to a canteloupe

ménagère, a basic preparation usually w/carrots, potatoes &/or onions (means "in the style of a housewife")

mendiants, dessert made of dry figs, raisins, almonds & nuts

menthe, mint

menthe poivrée, peppermint

menu, menu (often a fixed-price meal)

menu dégustation, set-price gourmet menu of specialties of the chef

Menu degustation is usually better Quality.

menu du jour, menu of the day

menu fixe, fixed-price menu

menu gastronomique, gourmet menu

menu pour enfant, children's menu

mer, sea

merda, *gnocchi* made w/Swiss chard

merenda, morning snack

merguez, spicy sausage (usually lamb)

meringues, baked shells of sweetened, beaten egg whites

merlan, whiting

merle, blackbird

Merle.

Merlot, dry, medium- to full-bodied red wine

merlu, a type of hake

merluche, dried cod

mérou, grouper

No thanks.

merveille, sugar doughnut

mesclun, lettuce salad of mixed greens

messine, an herb & cream sauce

méthode champenoise, sparkling wine (natural method)

mets, dish/preparation

mets selon la saison, seasonal preparation

meunière, w/parsley butter/seasoned fish floured & fried in butter, lemon & parsley. The word means "miller's wife" which refers to the flour that is used to prepare this dish

meurette, w/red wine sauce

Meursault, wine from Burgundy

miel, honey

miel Lavan

miettes, flakes/crumbs

mignardises, *petits fours* (small fancy cookies or cakes)

mignon, tenderloin cut

mignonette, small piece of fillet/coarsely ground white pepper

mijoté, simmered

milieu de poitrine, brisket

millas, corn-meal mush

mille-feuille, light pastry w/cream filling (napoleon)

millésime, vintage

mimolette, a mild cheese

mimosa, w/chopped egg yolks

mirabeau, w/anchovies & olives

mirabelle, yellow plum/plum brandy

mireilie, à la, there are many versions
  of this cold marinade

Mille feuille means a thousand leaves.

mirepoix, vegetables cut into cubes

miroir pommes, apple-Bavarian cream dessert

miroton, slices. Can also refer to a meat & onion stew or a
  brown sauce including onions

mitonnée, a souplike dish

mixte, mixed

mode, à la, in the style of

moelle, bone/marrow

moelleux, full-bodied. This can also mean tender

moka, coffee

mollusques, shellfish

momie, thimble-sized *pastis*

montagne, de, from the mountains

Mont Blanc, chestnut meringue topped w/a "mountain" of
  whipped cream (named after the mountain peak)

montmorency, w/cherries

morceau, piece

morille, morel mushroom (a rare,
  wild mushroom w/a smoky flavor)

morceau~ mor-so

mornay, white sauce w/cheese

mortadelle, bologna sausage
  w/pistachios & pickles

morue, salt cod

morue en rayte, cod in red wine sauce

moscovite, a dessert made in a mold w/any number of
  ingredients/a way of preparing duck

mouclade, creamy mussel soup

moule, mussel

moule de bouchot, small cultivated mussel

moule d'Espagne, large sharp-shelled mussel (frequently served raw)

moule de Parques, Dutch cultivated mussel

moules à la crème, mussels in white wine w/cream

moules à la poulette, mussels in a rich white wine sauce

moules marinières, mussels simmered in white wine w/shallots

mourtayrol, chicken dish flavored w/saffron

moussaka, a Greek dish frequently found on menus in Paris. It is an eggplant, lamb & tomato casserole

mousse, a light & airy dish of whipped cream or beaten egg whites/chopped meat or fish w/eggs & cream

mousse au chocolat, chocolate mousse

mousse de foie gras, *foie gras* must have, under French law, fattened liver w/up to 20% other foods. *Mousse de foie gras* contains up to 45% other foods such as eggs, pork liver &/or truffles

mousseline, w/whipped cream/*hollandaise* sauce w/cream

mousseron, small wild mushroom

mousseux, sparkling

moutarde, mustard

mouton, mutton

muge, mullet (in Provence)

mulet, mullet

munster, full-bodied cheese, often flavored w/caraway, cumin or anise)

mûre, blackberry

muscade, nutmeg

Muscadet, a dry, white wine

muscat, dessert wine

museau, muzzle

museau de veau, calf's muzzle

myrtille, blueberry

mystère, cooked meringue dessert w/ice cream

nage, "swimming;" served in an aromatic poaching liquid

nantua, crayfish or shrimp sauce

napolitaine, vanilla, strawberry & chocolate ice cream

nappe, tablecloth

nappé, covered in a sauce

nature, plain

muzzle... sounds grim.

myrtille ~ mir-tee.

naturel, plain. *Au naturel* means plainly cooked

navarin, mutton stew w/turnips

navet, turnip

nefle, small orange-colored fruit

nègre, flourless chocolate cake

neige, w/beaten egg whites (means "snow")

neufchâtel, rich, creamy cheese (a lower-fat cheese)

Newburg, lobster cooked in a sauce made of butter, cream,
   wine (or brandy) & egg yolks. Newburg is an alteration
   of Wenburg, the name of the patron for whom the
   sauce was named

niçoise, usually means w/tomatoes, anchovies, vinegar &
   black olives. Named after the city of Nice

nid d'abeilles, honey cake

nivernaise , à la, a dish w/carrots & onions

Noilly Prat, French vermouth

noir, black

noisette, hazelnut/round piece of meat

noix, nut/walnut. This can also refer to nuggets

noix d'acajou, cashew

noix de coco, coconut

noix de muscade, nutmeg

noix de pecan, pecan

noix de veau, top side of the leg of veal

non, not or no

nonats, tiny Mediterranean fish served deep fried

normande, usually means cooked w/fish, cream & mushrooms
   ("Normandy style"). This can also refer to a dish in a
   cream sauce often w/*calvados*

nougats, roasted almonds, egg whites, nuts & honey dessert

nouilles, noodles

nouilles fraîches maison, homemade fresh pasta

nouveau, new

nouveauté, new offering

nouvelle, new

noyau, pit (as in an olive pit)

Nuits-Saint-Georges, high-quality red wine from Burgundy

oeuf, egg. *Blancs d'oeufs* are egg whites
   & *jaunes d'oeufs* are egg yolks

oeuf à la coque, soft-boiled egg

oeuf à l'américaine, fried egg

Handwritten margin notes:

Navarin... I'll pass.

abeille– bee

Noisette can also mean a small cup of café crème.

Oeuf à la coque– egg in the shell.

oeuf à la russe, hard-boiled egg served
   cold w/diced vegetables in mayonnaise
oeuf à l'Huguenote, poached egg w/meat sauce
oeuf au plat, fried egg
oeuf brouillé, scrambled egg
oeuf chemise, poached egg
oeuf Côte d'Azur, poached egg in an artichoke bottom
oeuf dur, hard-boiled egg
oeuf dur soubise, hard-boiled egg w/onion & cream sauce
oeuf en gelée, poached egg served in gelatin
oeuf en meurette, poached egg in a red wine sauce
oeuf farci, stuffed egg
oeuf frit, fried egg
oeuf mayonnaise, eggs & mayonnaise
oeuf mollet, soft-boiled egg
oeuf poché, poached egg
oeuf poché à la Chartres, poached egg w/tarragon
oeuf Rossini, egg w/truffles & Madeira wine. This can also be a
   poached egg w/*pâté*
oeufs à la diable, devilled eggs
oeufs à la neige, whipped, sweetened egg whites served in a
   vanilla custard sauce (means "eggs in the snow")
oeufs au lait, egg custard
oeuf sauté à la poêle, fried egg
oeufs au vin, eggs poached in red wine
oeufs d'alose, cooked fish (shad) eggs
oeufs en meurette, poached eggs w/red wine sauce from
   Bourgogne
oeufs fermier, eggs from poultry raised on a farm
oeufs pochés suzettes, poached eggs in baked potatoes
oeuf sur la plat, fried egg
offert, free ("offered")
oie, goose
oie à l'instar de visé, goose boiled &
   then fried. A Belgian specialty
oignon, onion
oignons grelots, small pickled onions
oiseau, bird
olives, olives
olives farcies, stuffed olives
olives noires, black olives

Oie.

oiseau~
waZoe

olives vertes, green olives

omble-chevalier, freshwater fish of the trout family (char)

omelette, omelet

omelette au fromage, cheese omelet

omelette au jambon, ham omelet

omelette au lard, bacon omelet

omelette au naturel, plain omelet

omelette aux champignons, mushroom omelet

omelette aux fines herbs, omelet w/herbs

omelette brayaude, potato omelet

omelette César, omelet w/garlic & herbs

omelette complète, omelet w/ham & cheese

omelette fourée aux pommes dite à la Normande, apple upside-down cake

omelette landaise, omelet w/pine nuts

omelette nature, plain omelet

omelette norvégienne, baked Alaska

omelette parmentier, potato omelet

omelette paysanne, omelet w/bacon & potatoes

omelette quercynoise, cheese & walnut omelet

onglet, hanger steak

opéra, layered spongecake w/chocolate sauce

orange, orange

orange givrée, orange sorbet served in an orange

orange pressée, fresh, squeezed orange juice

oranges en rondelles, candied orange slices in orange jelly

oreilles, ears

oreillettes, pastry puffs

orge, barley

orgeat, almond-sugar syrup

origon, oregano

orties, nettles

ortolan, small game bird

os, bone

os à moelle, marrow bone

oseille, sorrel

ostendaise, w/shrimp & oysters

ou, or

ouassous, large crayfish found in the French West Indies

oursin, sea urchin

pacanes, pecans (in Guadeloupe)

Olives Farcies.

Ortolans are eaten whole, everything but the beak. They're illegal to serve.

paëlla, saffron-flavored rice & various ingredients. There are many variations of this famous Spanish dish found on menus all over France

pagre commun, sea bream

paillard, thin, flattened piece of meat, poultry or fish fillet

pailles pommes, fried, shredded potatoes

paillettes, cheese straws

pain, bread

pain au chocolat, chocolate-filled pastry

pain au lait, sweet bun

pain aux noix, walnut bread

pain aux raisins, bun w/custard & white raisins

pain blanc, white bread

pain complet, whole-wheat bread

pain de campagne, chewy "country" bread

pain de mie, sliced white bread (sandwich bread)

pain d'épices, gingerbread/a dense spice cake w/honey

pain de seigle, rye bread

pain de son, bran bread

pain de sucre, sugar loaf

pain grillé, toast

pain noir, dark bread

pain ordinaire, French bread

pain perdu, French toast. Literally, "lost bread" invented because French bread has no preservatives, thus becomes hard very quickly. The milk & eggs soften the bread

pain viennois, Vienna loaf

palaia, small sardines & anchovies

palais, cookies. *Palais de dames* are fruit cookies

paleron, shoulder of beef

paletot, skin, bone & meat of a fattened goose or duck (after the liver is removed)

palets de marrons, puréed-chestnut patties

palette de porc, pork shoulder

palmiers, palm hearts (*coeurs de palmier*). This can also refer to a caramelized puff pastry

paloise, *béarnaise* sauce w/mint

palombe, pigeon

palourdes, clams

pamplemousse, grapefruit

Pain ~
Pan

Bread is buttered at breakfast but not lunch or dinner.

Always liked that word.

panaché, mixed. *Un panaché* also refers to a drink made of half beer and half lemon soda

panade, thick mixture used to bind dumplings (panada)

panais, parsnip

pan bagnat, large round sandwich filled w/olive oil, onions, olives, tomatoes, anchovies & a hard-boiled egg. A specialty on the Côte d'Azur (means "wet bread"). This is a *salade niçoise* sandwich

pané, breaded

panier, basket

panisses, chickpea-flour pancake (deep fried)

panne de porc, fat from the kidneys of a pig

pannequet, rolled, filled crêpe

papalines, orange-flavored chocolates from Avignon

papeton d'aubergines, eggplant casserole from Avignon (means "eggplant of the popes")

papillons, butterfly cookies. This can also refer to a type of oyster

papillote, en, baked in parchment paper

paquets, en, in packages or parcels

parfait, ice-cream dessert. Can also refer to goose, duck or chicken-liver mousse

parfum, flavor

Paris-Brest, ring-shaped *éclair* filled w/praline cream

parisienne, a vegetable garnish w/potatoes sautéed in butter w/a white sauce

parme, amberjack (in Provence)

parmentier, dish containing potatoes

part, portion

partager, to share

passe-pierre, seaweed

Passe-Tout-Grain, red wine from Burgundy

pasta, pasta. Originally from neighboring Italy, pasta is an important part of Provençal cuisine

pastèque, watermelon

pastilles, hard, fruit- or mint-flavored candy

Pastèque.

pastis, anise-flavored aperitif. This is a Provençal word meaning mixture. It is a summer drink. Common brands are Pastis 51, Pernod, Ricard, Granier, Prado & Henri Bardouin

pastis landais, a sweet bread dessert

patate, sweet potato

patate douce, sweet potato

pâte, pastry dough.

> This can also mean a batter or paste.
> Do not confuse this w/*pâté* or *pâtes*

pâte à choux, cream-puff pastry

pâte à foncer, shortbread crust

pâte à frire, sweet french-frying batter

pâte à pain, bread dough

pâte brisée, pie pastry

pâte d'amandes, marzipan

pâte de fruits, fruit-paste candies

pâte feuilletée, puff pastry

pâte levée, bread dough

pâte sablée, sweet pie pastry

pâte sucrée, sweet pie pastry

pâté, pâté

pâté ardennais, purée of pork in a loaf of bread

pâté de campagne, *pâté* w/a variety of meats

pâté de canard, duck *pâté*

pâté de foie de volaille, chicken-liver *pâté*

pâté de foie d'oie, *pâté* that contains at least 50% goose liver &
> up to 50% other meats

pâté de foie gras, goose-liver *pâté*. Contains at least 75% goose
> liver

pâté doré, seasoned baked pork-liver *pâté* served cold

pâté en croûte, *pâté* in a pastry crust

pâté en pot, mutton soup found in the French West Indies

pâté maison et rillettes, a slice of a loaf of
> ground seasoned meat

pâtes, pasta

pâtisserie, pastry

patte, foot (paw) or leg of an animal or bird

patte blanche, small crayfish

patte rouge, large crayfish

Pauillac, rich red wine from Bordeaux

paupiette, slice of veal or beef
> rolled around stuffing

pavé, thick slice of beef (or calf's liver)

pavé aux marrons, chestnut & chocolate cake

pavot, graines de, poppy seeds

Pâte is pastry.
Pâté is pâté.
Pâtes is pasta.

Patte blanche.

paysanne, à la, "country style" usually means a dish containing assorted vegetables

pays d'auge, cream & cider sauce

pays, du, from the area

peau, skin

pêche, peach

pêche melba, peaches w/ice cream & raspberry sauce

pêcheur, this term refers to fish preparations (means "fisherman")

pelardons, goat cheese

pelé, peeled

pelure, peelings

perce-pierre, seaweed

perche, perch

perdreau, young partridge

perdrix, partridge

périgourdine, à la, w/goose- or duck-liver purée & truffles

périgueux, a brown sauce w/chopped truffles

Pernod, anise-flavored aperitif

perroquet, a drink of *pastis* & mint

persil, parsley. *Persillé* means parslied

persillade, chopped parsley & garlic

pesto, see *pistou*

pétillant, slightly sparkling beverage

petit, small

petit beurre, tea biscuit

petit déjeuner, breakfast

petite friture, fried whitebait

petit four, small fancy cookie or cake

petit gâteau, small cake/cookie

petit-gris, small snail

petit noir, black coffee

petit pain, roll. *Petits pains au maïs* are made w/corn meal

petit pois, pea

petit pois de cérons, peas w/pork

petit salé, salt pork

petits farcis provençaux, stuffed vegetables of Provence

petits gâteaux, cookies

petits pois, peas

petits pois à la Normande, creamed peas

petit-suisse, creamy, unsalted cheese/cheese *beignets*

pétoncle, tiny scallop
pets de nonne, small fried pastry
pibale, small eel
pichet, pitcher of wine
picodon, goat's-milk cheese from Provence
picon bière, beer mixed w/a sweet liqueur
pièce, piece/each
pied, foot
pied de cochon, pig's foot
pied de mouton, wild mushroom/sheep's foot
pied de porc, pig's foot
pieps et paquets, stuffed-tripe dish
pietra, chestnut-flavored beer from Corsica
pieuvre, octopus
pigeon, pigeon
pigeonneau, young pigeon
pignatelle, small cheese fritter
pignons, pine nuts/croissant w/pine nuts
pilaf/pilau, rice cooked w/broth & onions
piment, chili pepper/pimento
piment doux, sweet pepper
piment en poudre, chili powder
piment poivre de Jamaïque, allspice
pimprenelle, burnet (a green used in salads)
pince, claw
pineau, cognac & grape juice
pintade, guinea hen
pintadeau, young guinea hen
pipérade, omelet w/ham, green peppers, tomatoes & garlic
piquant, spicy hot
piquante, sauce of pickles or capers, shallots & vinegar
piqué, larded
pissala, fish purée used in *pissaladière*
pissaladière, pizza-like tart w/onions,
    black olives & purée of anchovies
    & sardines (from Provence)
pissenlit, dandelion leaves
pistache, pistachio
pistil de safran, thread of saffron
pistou, garlic, basil, nuts & olive oil sauce (known as pesto in
    Italy)/pesto soup

pichet.

Pee-shay.

Piment doux

Never warmed up to this

pithiviers, puff pastry filled w/ground almonds & sweet cream

pizza, pizza is not shared in France, is not eaten w/your hands & will be served w/a bottle of olive oil w/hot peppers at the bottom. The oil is to spice up your pizza. A cheese & tomato pizza is called a ***marguerite***

pizza quatres saisons, four-seasons pizza (four toppings: ham, mushrooms, cheese & anchovy)

pizza reine, pizza topped w/ham & mushrooms

planteurs, rum & fruit punches found in the French West Indies

plaque de chocolat, chocolate bar

plat, plate/dish

plat de résistance, main course

plat du jour, plate (special) of the day

plate, flat-shelled oyster. This can also refer to water w/out carbonation

plateau, platter

plateau de fromages, platter of cheeses. In Normandy, this is almost always served w/*calvados*

plat froid, cold plate

plat minceur, diet plate

plat principal (plats principaux), main course(s)

pleurote, grey mushroom found in the Loire Valley

plie, flounder/plaice

plie franche, flounder

plombières, vanilla ice-cream dessert w/whipped cream & candied fruit

pluviers, plovers (small birds)

poché, poached

pochouse, fish & onion stew prepared w/wine (from Bourgogne)

poêle, à la, fried

point, à, medium done. In France, this means still pink

pointe, tip. ***Pointe d'asperge*** is an asparagus tip

poire, pear

poireau (poireaux), leek(s)

poire Belle Hélène, pear w/ice cream & chocolate sauce

poirier d'anjou, pear cake

Plat minceur. I hope you're just looking this up to see what it is, not ordering it!

Plie.

A poêle is a frying pan.

pois, peas
pois chiche, chick-pea
pois mange-tout, snow pea
poisson, fish
poisson à grande friture, deep-dried fish
poisson d'eau douce, freshwater fish
poisson de mer, saltwater fish
poissonnerie, fish soup/fish store
poitrine, breast
poitrine d'agneau Sainte Menehould, braised & grilled
    lamb breast
poitrine demi-sel, slab of unsmoked bacon
poitrine de mouton, mutton breast
poitrine de porc, pork belly
poitrine de veau, veal breast
poitrine fumée, slab of smoked bacon
poivrade, brown sauce of wine, vegetables, peppers & vinegar
poivre, pepper. *Au poivre* means w/peppercorns
poivre d'Ain, flavored *banon* (cheese)
poivre d'ane, bitter, peppery herb
poivre de cayenne, very hot red pepper
poivre de Chine, mouth-numbing type of peppercorn
poivre de la Jamaïque, allspice (the main ingredient of jerk
    seasoning)
poivre frais de Madagascar, green peppercorns
poivre mignonette, crushed peppercorns used on steaks
poivre noir, black peppercorns
poivre rose, pink peppercorns
poivre vert, green peppercorns
poivron, bell pepper
poivron doux, sweet bell pepper
poivron épicé, hot pepper
poivron rouge, red pepper
poivron vert, green pepper
polenta, corn meal/polenta (dish of
    boiled corn meal, w/butter & cheese)
Pomerol, a red wine (merlot) from Bordeaux
pommade, a thick paste
pomme, apple
pomme au four, potato baked in its skin
pomme bonne femme, baked apple

poisson.

*au four
litehally
"in the oven"*

pomme de terre, potato

pomme de terre brayaude, oven-cooked potato

pomme en l'air, caramelized apple slices
served w/blood sausage

pommes à l'anglaise, boiled potatoes

pommes allumettes, very thin french fries

pommes anna, sliced potato & cheese dish

pommes boulangère, a potato &
meat dish/sliced potatoes w/onions

pommes château, potatoes fried in butter

pommes dauphine, potatoes mashed in
butter & egg yolks, mixed in flour
& deep fried

Most of the time pomme refers to potato though it means apple... sorry can't be more specific.

pommes dauphinoise, potatoes baked w/garlic, cheese & milk

pommes de terre à la berrichonne, herbed potatoes

pommes de terre à l'angoumois, potato & cabbage casserole

pommes duchesse, potatoes mashed in butter & egg yolks

pommes en robe de chambre, potatoes in their skin

pommes en robe des champs, potatoes in their skin

pommes fondantes, potatoes cooked in butter

pommes frites, french fries

pommes gratinées, potatoes baked w/cheese

pommes lyonnaises, potatoes sautéed w/onions

pommes mousseline, mashed potatoes

pommes nature, boiled or steamed potatoes

pommes nouvelles, new potatoes

pommes paille, fried strips of potatoes

pommes Pont-Neuf, french fries

Pommes frites, one of the miraculous joys of France.

pommes renversées, baked caramelized apple pudding

pommes sautées, fried potatoes

pommes soufflées, puffy slices of potatoes fried twice

pommes vapeur, steamed or boiled potatoes

pompe à l'huile, sweet flat bread flavored w/olive oil

pont l'évêque, strong, flavored, semi-hard cheese (usually
served in square blocks)

porc, pork

porc au lait, pork cooked in milk

porc aux deux pommes, pork w/potatoes & apples

porc demi-sel, salted pork

porcelet, young suckling pig

porchetta/porketta, an Italian dish of roast, stuffed suckling pig

porc salé, salted pork

Porto, port

porto, au, w/port

port-salut/port du salut, mild, soft, buttery cheese

portugaises, a type of oyster

potable, drinkable

potage, soup (usually thick)

potage à la crème de coco, cream-of-coconut soup found in the French West Indies

potage au cerfeuil, soup of chervil & other herbs. A specialty in the Ardennes region of Belgium

potage bilbi, fish & oyster soup

potage bonne femme, potato & leek soup

potage cancalais, fish soup

potage Crécy, carrot soup

potage crème normande, cream of fish soup

potage cressonière, watercress soup

potage cultivateur, soup w/mixed vegetables & pork

potage d'Auvergne, lentil & potato soup

potage du Père Tranquille, lettuce soup

potage du Barry, cauliflower soup

potage Longchamp, soup featuring peas

potage nivernaise, carrot soup

potage parmentier, leek & potato soup

potage portugais, tomato *potage*

potage printanier, vegetable soup

potage Saint-Germain, split-pea soup

potage soissonnais, haricot-bean soup

potage velouté, creamy soup

pot-au-feu, stew of meat & vegetables

pot-de-crème, mousse or custard dessert

potée, boiled pork (or beef) w/cabbage

pothine de boeuf, beef braised w/*calvados*. The *pothine* is a cast-iron casserole in which this dish is cooked

potiron, pumpkin

Pouilly-Fuissé, dry white wine from Burgundy

poularde, capon/fatted chicken

poularde Sainte-Hélène, chicken w/dumplings

poule, hen

poule au pot, stewed chicken w/vegetables

poule au riz, hen served w/rice

potage.

poule d'Inde, turkey hen

poule faisane, pheasant

poule farcie en daube à la berrichonne, boned, stuffed chicken in jelly.

NOT crazy about jellied meat.

poulet, chicken

poulet basquaise, chicken w/sweet peppers & tomatoes ("Basque style")

poulet Biarritz, chicken in white wine

poulet chasseur, chicken usually w/mushrooms & white wine. This can also be chicken in tomato sauce

poulet.

poulet créole, chicken in a white sauce (often spicy) & served w/rice

poulet de Bresse, free-range, corn-fed chicken

poulet de grain, corn-fed chicken. Sold in shops with a special ring around its "foot" to prove they are authentic.

poulet de Saint-Astier, chicken stew

poulet fermier, free-range chicken

poulet Marengo, chicken cooked in white wine w/tomatoes, garlic, mushrooms & shallots. Said to be the chicken dish served to Napoleon after the battle of Marengo in 1800

poulet rôti, roast chicken

poulpe, octopus

poulpe.

pourboire, tip

pour/à emporter, to go/take out

pourpier, purslane (a green used in

pousse-pierre, seaweed

poussin, spring chicken

praire, clam

praline, caramelized almonds

premier cru, denotes a high-quality wine

pré-salé, lambs that graze on salt meadows

pressé, fresh squeezed

presse, à la, pressed

pression, draft beer.
   À la pression means from the tap

primeur, early season or spring fruits & vegetables

Prince-de-Galles, stuffed w/*pâté*

printanière, à la, w/spring vegetables

prisuttu, cured ham from Corsica

prix, price

prix fixe, fixed price

prix net, service is included

profiteroles, little cream puffs filled w/ice
cream & covered in chocolate sauce

Profiteroles ~ food of the gods.

provençale, à la, w/garlic, onions, herbs & tomatoes
("Provence style"). Provence is one of
France's wine-growing regions and, of course,
one of the world's best-known &
loved tourist destinations

prune, plum

pruneau/pruneau sec, prune

pudding, custard/pudding

puits d'amour, pastry filled w/custard

pulenta, chestnut-flour bread from Corsica

purée, strained fruit or vegetables.
En purée means mashed

purée de pommes de terre, mashed potatoes

pyramide au chocolat, chocolate pyramid filled w/chocolate
pieces & sauces, whipped cream & butter

quartiers d'orange glacés, caramelized orange sections. A
dessert found on menus in Provence

quart, un, on a menu this denotes a quarter-liter of wine

quatre-épices, a blend of four spices
(nutmeg, cloves, ginger &
white pepper)

quatre-quarts, a cake made from
four ingredients – eggs, flour,
butter & sugar – of equal weight.
A specialty in Brittany

quatre-quarts is like pound cake.

quenelle, dumpling

quenelles de foie de veau, calf's-liver dumplings. A specialty in
Luxembourg

quetsche, small plum/liquor made from plums

queue, tail

queue de boeuf, oxtail

quiche, egg tart w/vegetable, seafood or meat filling

quiche au fromage blanc, bacon & white cheese *quiche*

quiche lorraine, *quiche* w/cheese, bacon & onions

râble, loin of rabbit

râble de lièvre, saddle of rabbit

racasse, scorpion fish

raclette, cheese heated until it begins to melt. The melted part is scraped off & placed on a warm plate to be eaten w/boiled potatoes, pickles & pickled onions. This can also refer to melted cheese on a *baguette*

radis, radish

radis.

radis noir, large black radish

ragoût, stewed/meat stew

raie, ray/skate (fish)

raifort, horseradish

raisin, grape(s)

raisins de Corinthe, currants

raisins.

raisins de table, dessert grapes

raisin sec, raisin(s)

raïto, red wine, tomato & onion sauce

ramequin, small cheese tart or a small casserole

rancio, dessert wine

râpé, shredded/grated. *La râpée* is a creamed-potato pancake

rascasse, fish found in the Mediterranean (scorpion fish)

ratatouille, eggplant casserole

rave, root vegetable

ravigote, vinegar dressing (w/herbs & shallots)

ravioli, ravioli. Common in Nice & all of the French Riviera

reblochon, soft, strong cheese

à la reine...
of the
queen.

refroidi, chilled

régional(e), from the region/local

reine, à la, w/mince meat or poultry

reine-claude, small green or yellow plums (greengage)

reinette, fall & winter apple

religieuse, *éclair* pastry. This pastry got its name because it looks like a nun in her habit

rémoulade, mayonnaise sauce

renversée, turned out of its cooking container

repas, meal

Rhône, this valley is one of France's wine regions (located in South Central France) & known for its white and red wines

rhubarbe, rhubarb

rhum, rum

Ricard, anise-flavored aperitif

Richelieu, à la, w/tomatoes, bacon & potatoes

rigotte, goat cheese

rillettes, highly seasoned meat baked in its own fat (potted meat)

rillons, pork belly
ris, sweetbreads
ris d'agneau, lamb sweetbreads
ris de..., sweetbreads
ris de veau, veal sweetbreads (the pancreas of a veal calf)
rissole, pastry/meat or fish patty
rissolé, fried until brown & crisp
riz, rice. *Crème de riz* is rice flour
    (very finely gound rice)
riz à l'impératrice, rice pudding
riz basquais, spicy rice
riz complet, brown rice
rizotto, risotto
riz pilaf, rice boiled in bouillon w/onions (rice pilaf)
riz safrané, saffron rice
riz sauvage, wild rice
robe des champs, en, in its skin
Robert, a brown sauce w/onions, white wine & mustard
rocambole, a member of the onion family
rognon, kidney
rognonnade, veal loin
rognons blancs, testicles
rognons de veau à la liégeoise, roast veal kidneys
romarin, rosemary
romsteck, rump steak
rondelle, round slice
roquefort, blue cheese
roquette, arugula (rocket)
rosbif, roast beef
rosé, rosé. This can also refer to rare meat
rosette, dried sausage/small round piece
Rossini, a dish that includes *foie gras* & truffles
rôti, roast/roasted
rouelle, a slice cut at an angle
rouelle de veau, veal shank
rouge, red
rouget, red mullet
rouille, spicy sauce of peppers, garlic & tomatoes
rouilleuse, red garlic mayonnaise
roulade, rolled slice of meat or fish w/stuffing/"Swiss roll"
    dessert w/cream or jam stuffing

Handwritten notes:
ris - ree
riz - ree
Don't get 'em mixed up.

Rognon ~ runyun

Pass on the entire Rongum selection

Rouget.

roulé, rolled
rouleau, roll of...
roussillonnade, grilled sausage & mushroom dish
roux, flour & butter mixture (used to thicken sauces or soup)
rouzoles, crêpes filled w/bacon & ham
rumsteck, rump steak
sabayon, creamy dessert of wine, sugar, egg yolks &
    flavoring/cream wine sauce
sablé, shortbread cookie
saccharine, saccharin
sachet de thé, tea bag
safran, saffron
saignant, very rare
saindoux, pork fat
Saint-Amour, red wine from Beaujolais
Saint-Emilion, red wine form Bordeaux
Saint-Estèphe, red wine from Bordeaux
Saint-Germain, w/peas
Saint-Honoré, cake w/cream
Saint-Hubert, sauce w/bacon & chestnuts
Saint-Jacques, sea scallop
Saint-Julien, red wine from Bordeaux
Saint-Marcellin, goats' or cows' cheese w/a smoky flavor
Saint-Raphaël, quinine-flavored aperitif
Saint-Paulin, mild, semi-soft cheese
Saint-Pierre, John Dory fish (a firm-textured, white-fleshed fish
    w/a mild, sweet flavor and low fat content)
saison, season
salade, salad
salade antiboise, salad usually w/fish, capers & green peppers
salade au bleu, salad w/blue cheese (& frequently walnuts)
salade au chapon, salad served on toast rubbed w/garlic
salade aux noix, green salad w/walnuts
salade cauchoise, ham, potato & celery salad
salade chiffonnade, shredded lettuce & sorrel
salade composée, chef's salad
salade d'Auvergne, salad w/blue cheese dressing
salade de boulghour, bulgur wheat salad
salade de crudités, chopped vegetable salad
salade de fruits, fruit cocktail
salade de gésiers, green salad w/gizzards

*St. Emilion—
personal
favorite.*

*Chapon refers
to the toast.*

salade de liège, bean & potato salad. A specialty in Belgium
salade de museau de boeuf, marinated beef headcheese
salade de saison, seasonal salad
salade de tomates, tomato salad
salade folle, mixed salad usually w/green beans

Salade folle ~ crazy salad

salade lyonnaise, *hors d'oeuvre* of seasoned meats in an oil, shallot & vinegar dressing
salade mélangée, mixed salad
salade mêlée, mixed salad
salade mesclun, mixed greens
salade mixte, mixed salad
salade multicolore, salad w/radishes, peppers, egg, cucumber, corn & basil
salade niçoise, salad usually w/tomatoes, anchovies or tuna, potatoes, vinegar & black olives (served as a main course)
salade panachée, mixed salad
salade paysanne, salad w/eggs & pieces of bacon
salade russe, diced vegetables in mayonnaise
salade simple, green salad
salade verte, green salad
salade wallonie, warm salad w/lettuce, bacon & fried potatoes. A specialty in Belgium
salaisons, an hors d'oeuvre of olives, anchovies &/or herring
salé, salted
salicorne, algae used as a condiment
salmis, roasted game or poultry
salpicon, stuffing w/sauce
salsifis, salsify (oyster plant)

Salpicon – like the word and the concept!

Sancerre, white & pale, light-bodied red wines from the Loire Valley
sandre, pike
sandwich, sandwich
sandwich au fromage, cheese sandwich
sandwich au jambon, ham sandwich
sandwich au saucisson, dried-sausage sandwich
sandwich aux rillettes, *pâté* sandwich
sandwich crudités, lettuce &/or chopped vegetable sandwich
sang, blood
sanglier, wild boar

Sanglier. A specialty in the Ardennes.

sans, without
sans arêtes, boneless
sans peau, skinless
sarcelle, teal (river duck)
sardine, sardine
sarrasin, buckwheat
sarriette, summer savory (an herb)
sartando, small fried fish w/hot vinegar
sartenais, hard, strong cheese from Corsica
sauce, sauce/gravy/salad dressing
sauce à la crème, cream sauce
sauce aurore, a white sauce w/tomato purée
sauce aux câpres, a white sauce w/capers
sauce bigarade, orange sauce
sauce bretonne, egg, butter & mustard sauce
sauce café de Paris, cream, mustard & herb sauce
sauce catalane, tomato, orange & garlic sauce
sauce gaillarde, seasoned mayonnaise
sauce mornay, cheese sauce
sauce poulette, mushroom, egg yolk & wine sauce
sauce soubise, onion sauce
sauce Suzette, orange sauce
sauce veloutée, creamy soup/white sauce (*roux* mixed w/poultry,
   fish, veal or mushroom stock)
sauce vinot, wine sauce
saucisse, sausage
saucisse à l'ail tiède, garlic sausage
   (served warm)
saucisse à la navarraise, sausage w/wine
   & sweet peppers
saucisse de Francfort, hot dog/frankfurter
saucisse de Strasbourg, beef sausage
saucisse de Toulouse, fresh pork sausage
saucisson, dried sausage
saucisson à l'alsacienne, poached sausage w/horseradish sauce
saucisson à la lyonnaise, poached sausage w/potato salad
saucisson chaud de Lyon en croûte, red sausage w/cubes of
   fat & baked in pastry
saucisson de Lyon, dried seasoned sausage
sauge, sage
saumon, salmon

[handwritten notes in right margin:]
Saucisse ~
Sausage like
bratwurst
Saucisson ~
Sausage like
Salami

Sauge.

saumon de l'Atlantique, Atlantic salmon

saumon fumé, smoked salmon

Saumur-Champigny, light-bodied red wine from the
    Loire Valley

saupiquet, spicy cream sauce w/bread crumbs

saupiquet des amognes, ham w/spicy cream sauce

sauté, sautéed

Sauternes, a fruity white dessert wine

sauvage, wild

Sauvignon de Touraine, white wine from the
    Sauvignon Blanc grape

savarin, spongecake topped w/rum & cream

Savoie, one of France's wine-growing regions

savoyarde, flavored w/cheese. *À la savoyarde* also can refer to
    a vermouth & cream sauce

scampi, prawns

scarole, escarole, a salad green (a type of *endive*)

scotch, scotch

sec, dry/straight

séché, dried

seiche, large squid/cuttlefish

seiches farcies, cuttlefish stuffed w/a mixture of sausage
    & the meat of cuttlefish tentacles

seigle, rye

sel, salt

sel-épicé, salt spiced w/basil, nutmeg, cloves, cinnamon,
    peppercorns, bay leaves & coriander

sel gemme, rock salt

sel gris, coarse rock or sea salt

selle, saddle of meat, generally the loin roast

selle anglaise, saddle of meat

sel marin, sea salt

selon arrivage, on a menu, this means the dish
    depends on availability

selon grandeur/selon grosseur, price paid by the size or weight

sel raffiné, refined salt

semoule, semolina flour

sériole, amber jack, a type of fish

serpolet, wild thyme

serran, perch

service compris, service included

service non compris, service not include

serviette, napkin

s.g., abbreviation for price paid by the size or weight

sherry, sherry

sirop, syrup

sirop de sucre d'érable, maple syrup

smitane, cream, wine & onion sauce

socca, *crêpe* made w/chickpea flour served on the Côte d'Azur

soissons, white beans

soja, soy

sole, sole

sole normande, sole in a butter, onion, mushroom, white wine, cream & *calvados* sauce

son, bran

sorbet, sherbet

soubise, onion sauce

soubise-aurore, onion & tomato sauce

soucoupe, saucer

soufflé, soufflé (beaten egg whites w/various ingredients baked in a mold)

soufflé à la reine, soufflé w/poultry or meat

soufflé au Grand Marnier, soufflé w/orange liqueur

soufflé Rothschild, vanilla-flavored fruit soufflé

soupe, soup

soupe à l'oignon gratinée, French onion soup

soupe au pistou, vegetable & noodle soup (soup w/pesto found in the South of France)

soupe corse, Corsican soup of vegetables & herbs simmered w/a ham bone

soupe de montagne, Corsican soup of vegetables & herbs simmered w/a ham bone

soupe de poisson, fish soup

soupe paysanne, Corsican soup of vegetables & herbs simmered w/a ham bone

soupe pêcheur, fish soup

spaghetti, spaghetti

spats, small fish of the herring family

spécialité, specialty

spécialité de la maison, house specialty

spécialité du chef, chef's specialty

spécialités locales, local dishes

steak, steak

steak au poivre, steak topped w/crushed peppercorns. ***Steak au poivre vert*** is steak in a green-peppercorn sauce & ***steak au poivre rouge*** is steak in a red-peppercorn sauce

steak frites, steak & french fries

steak haché, hamburger

steak tartare, raw hamburger or chopped beef (usually topped w/a raw egg)

stockfish, niçoise spicy fish stew

stufatu, Corsican stew w/pasta

succès au pralin, meringue cake w/almonds

sucettes, lollipops ("suckers")

suchi, sushi

sucre, sugar

sucre candi, candy sugar

sucre de canne roux, brown sugar

sucre filé, spun sugar

Sucre filé is found adorning Croquemboche.

suprême, chicken-based sauce/breast of chicken or game or fillet of fish w/an unusual combination of ingredients

suprême de volaille, chicken breast. Usually a boned chicken breast in a creamy sauce

sur commande, to your special order

surgelé(s), frozen food

surlonge, beef chuck roast

sus, en, in addition. ***Boisson en sus*** means drink not included

Suze, an aperitif flavored w/gentian, an herb

tablier de sapeur, grilled breaded tripe

tagine/tajine, stew (lamb, veal or chicken) w/vegetables. This spicy stew is a specialty in North Africa (especially Morocco). Also a clay cooking vessel

Tagine.

tanche, the freshwater fish tench

tapenade, mixture of black olives, olive oil, lemon juice, capers & anchovies (a spread from Provence)

tarama, mullet-roe spread

tartare, chopped raw beef/in a salad, this refers to a mayonnaise-based sauce

Tanche.

tarte, pie/tart

tarte à l'oignon, onion & cream tart

tarte alsacienne, apple & custard tart

tarte au citron meringuée, lemon meringue pie

tarte au fruit, fruit tart

tartelette, small tart

tarte tatin, upside-down apple tart. Legend has it that this tart was "created" when the Tatin sisters (who operated a restaurant) put the tart in the oven & left for church. They discovered their mistake, turned it upside down & served it.

tarte tropézienne, yellow cake w/custard filling (created by a Polish baker in 1955 in St Tropez)

tartine, open-faced sandwich (half baguette w/butter)

tasse, cup

Tavel, rosé wine from the Côte du Rhône region

The luscious-sounding Tartine buerré is nothing more than buttered bread.

tendre, tender

tendre de tranche, round steak

tendron, breast

tendron de veau, veal breast

terrine, *pâté*/prepared in an earthenware dish

terrine de campagne, pork & liver *pâté*

terrine de légumes, ground & seasoned vegetable loaf

terrinée, caramel-rice pudding

tête, head

tête de veau vinaigrette, calf's head w/vinegar & oil dressing

teurgoule, caramel-rice pudding

thé, tea

thé au lait, tea w/milk

Not on your life!

thé citron, tea w/ lemon

thé glacé, iced tea

thé nature, tea w/out milk

thon, tuna

thon mirabeau, tuna cooked in eggs & milk

thym, thyme

tian, a dish (usually rice, vegetables & cheese) cooked in an oval-shaped earthenware dish used on the Côte d'Azur

tian de Saint-Jacques et légumes provençal, sea scallops on a bed of chopped vegetables

tiède, lukewarm

tilleul, herb tea

timbale, cup. *En timbale* means meat, fish or fruit in a mold

ti punch, rum, lime & sugarcane syrup drink found in the French West Indies

'Ti means petit

tisane, herbal tea

toast, toast (little pieces of crispy bread)

tomate, tomato. This also is the name for
a drink of *pastis* mixed w/grenadine

Tomate

tomates à la provençal, baked tomatoes stuffed w/bread
crumbs, garlic & parsley

tomates concassées, roughly chopped tomatoes

tomates farcies, tomatoes stuffed w/seasoned bread crumbs

tomme (or tome) au marc, the crust of this smooth & creamy
cheese is made of grape pulp. Also known as *fondu aux
raisins*

tomme (de Savoie), soft, mild cheese

tonique, tonic

tonneaux en chêne, oak barrels

Tortue.

topinambour, Jerusalem artichoke

tortue, turtle

tortue véritable, turtle soup

toulousaine, usually means served w/sweetbreads or truffles
("Toulouse style")

tourain, bread & garlic soup

tourin bordelais, French onion soup (usually w/bread on the
bottom of the bowl)

tournedos, round cut of prime steak

tournedos Rossini, *tournedos* served w/Madeira wine sauce &
served w/*foie gras* &/or truffles

Tourteau.

tourta da blea, Swiss chard pie

tourte, pie

tourteau, large crab

tourte aux blettes, sweet tart of eggs,
cheese, raisins, pine nuts & chard

tourte du jour, savory pie of the day

tourtière, pastry filled w/prunes &/or apples.
Also the name for a cooking dish

tourton, pastry filled w/prunes, apples, spinach & garlic

tout compris, everything is included in the price

tout épice, allspice

tranche, slice. *Tranché* means sliced

tranche grasse, sirloin tip

tranche napolitaine, slice of layered ice cream

travers de porc, spareribs

treipen, black pudding & sausages w/potatoes

très, very
trifle, trifle
tripe, tripe
tripe à la luxembourgeoise, tripe
    specialty found in Luxembourg

Remember the general rule about Tripe... dont.

tripes à la mode, tripe in butter, onions & *calvados.*
    A popular dish in Normandy
tripes à la mode de Caen, tripe baked w/calf's feet
tripes à la mode narbonnaise, tripe in tomato sauce
Triple Sec, orange liqueur
tripoux, mutton tripe
trompettes des morts, wild mushrooms
tronçon, large slice of meat or fish
trouchia, trout. In Provence, this refers to an omelet
truffat, potato-cream pie
truffe, truffle. *Truffé* means w/truffles. Truffles are extremely
    expensive wild fungi that grow around the roots of trees.
    They must be "sniffed out" by pigs or dogs. *Truffes* also
    refers to chocolate truffles
truffettes dauphinoise, chocolate truffles
truite, trout
truite à l'ardennaise, Belgian dish of
    trout cooked in a wine sauce

Truite.

truite au bleu, poached trout
truite meunière, trout in a parsley & butter sauce
truite saumonée, salmon trout
ttoro, Basque mixed-fish dish
tuile, almond cookie
turbon, ingredients cooked in a ring mold
turbot, turbot, a fish
turbotin, small turbot
vacherin, mellow Swiss cheese
vacherin glacée, baked meringue dessert
valençay, goat's-milk cheese
Vallée d'Ange, w/cooked apples & cream (named after a region
    in Normandy)
vanille, vanilla
vanneau, small bird
vapeur, steamed
varié/variés, assorted
veau, veal

veau Marengo, veal w/garlic, tomatoes, white wine & cognac
végétarien/végétarienne, vegetarian
velouté, creamy soup/white sauce
    (*roux* mixed w/poultry, fish,
    veal or mushroom stock)
velouté d'asperges, creamy white asparagus soup
venaison, venison
ventre, stomach/belly
ventrèche, salted & seasoned pork belly
vénus, clam
verdures, green salad vegetables
verjus, the juice of unripened grapes
vermicelle, tiny, thin noodles used in soup
vermouth, vermouth
vernis, large clam
verre, glass
vert, green/a sauce of spinach,
    mayonnaise & herbs
vert-pré, watercress garnish
verveine, the herbal tea lemon verbena
vessie, cooked in a pig's bladder
viande, meat
viande séchée, thin slices of cured beef
viandes froides, cold meats
vichy, w/glazed carrots
vichyssoise, cold leek & potato soup
vieille, old
vieille cure, wine-distilled liqueur
vieille prune, plum-based *eau-de-vie*
vierge beurre, a simple butter sauce w/lemon juice, salt & pepper
vierge huile d'olive, virgin olive oil
vieux, old
vigneronne, sauce w/grapes & wine
vigne, sarments de, vine cuttings used w/grilled foods
vin, wine
vinaigre, vinegar
vinaigre balsamique, balsamic vinegar
vinaigre de vin, wine vinegar
vinaigrette, generally a salad dressing
    of vinegar, mustard, herbs & oil
vin blanc, white wine

Verjus is sometimes used instead of vinegar.

Une verre de vin rouge

Vielle cure means remedy... An excuse to drink...

Vin is pronounced Van with just a hint of the 'N'.

vin chambré, wine served at room temperature

vin cuit, sweet dessert wine

Vin Délimité de Qualité Supérieure (VDQS), denotes a local wine made according to strict standards

vin de maison, house wine

vin de paille, straw wine w/a strong flavor & aroma

vin de pays, wine guaranteed to originate in a certain region ("country wine")

vin de table, table wine

vin de xérès, sherry

vin doux, sweet wine/dessert wine

vin doux naturel, naturally sweet wine

vin du pays, local wine

vin gris, pink wine

vin jaune, yellow wine

vin liquoreux, sweet wine

vin mousseux, sparkling wine

vin nouveau, new wine

vin ordinaire, table wine

vin rosé, rosé wine

vin rouge, red wine

vin sec, dry wine

The French don't fill their glasses more than halfway

violet de Provence, braid of garlic

violette, crystallized violet petals

vivant/vivante, alive/living

vodka, vodka

volaille, poultry

Volaille~
Voe-Lie.

vol-au-vent, puff pastry filled w/fish, meat &/or sweetbreads

waterzooi, chicken or fish poached in a sauce w/vegetables. A Belgian specialty

waterzooi de poulet, chicken poached in a sauce w/vegetables

whisky, whisky

Williamine, a pear brandy

xérès, sherry

yaourt/yogourt, yogurt

Yvorne, a dry Swiss white wine

zeste, citrus zest

zeste de citron, lemon zest

zeste de citron confits, candied lemon zest

zeste d'orange, orange zest

zewelwai, onion & cream tart from Alsace

Descriptions of restaurants listed here can be found on the
page number following each listing.

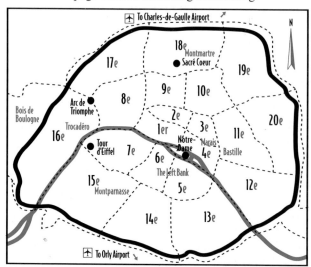

RESTAURANT AND FOOD NOTES

RESTAURANT AND FOOD NOTES

Informative, Opinionated, Fun

The best menu translator/restaurant guides avai
Handy, pocket-sized ... a must for all travelers

www.eatndrink.com

Published by Open Road Publishing
Distributed by Simon & Schuster